GROVE PRESS MODERN DRAMATISTS

Grove Press Modern Dramatists

Series Editors: *Bruce King* and *Adele King*

Published titles

Further titles in preparation

GROVE PRESS MODERN DRAMATISTS

AMERICAN DRAMATISTS 1918–1945

Bernard F. Dukore
Professor of Drama and Theatre at
the University of Hawaii

Grove Press, Inc., New York

First published in 1984 by
Higher and Further Education Division
MACMILLAN PUBLISHERS LTD
London and Basingstoke

First Grove Press Hardcover Edition 1984
First Printing 1984
ISBN: 0-394-54293-2

First Evergreen Edition 1984
First Printing 1984
ISBN: 0-394-62340-1

Printed in Great Britain

GROVE PRESS, INC., 196 West Houston Street,
New York, NY 10014

5 4 3 2 1

Contents

List of Plates

vi

Acknowledgements

The author and publisher are grateful to the following for permission to reproduce photographs: The Theatre Collection, Museum of the City of New York for plates 5, 6, 7 and 9; The Billy Rose Theatre Collection of the New York Public Library at Lincoln Center for plates 1, 2, 3, 4, 8, 10 and 11.

Editors' Preface

The *Grove Press Modern Dramatists* is an international series of introductions to major and significant nineteenth and twentieth century dramatists, movements and new forms of drama in Europe, Great Britain, America and new nations such as Nigeria and Trinidad. Besides new studies of great and influential dramatists of the past, the series includes volumes on contemporary authors, recent trends in the theatre and on many dramatists, such as writers of farce, who have created theatre 'classics' while being neglected by literary criticism. The volumes in the series devoted to individual dramatists include a biography, a survey of the plays, and detailed analysis of the most significant plays, along with discussion, where relevant, of the political, social, historical and theatrical context. The authors of the volumes, who are involved with theatre as playwrights, directors, actors, teachers and critics, are concerned with the plays as theatre and discuss such matters as performance, character interpretation and staging, along with themes and contexts.

BRUCE KING
ADELE KING

Preface

'Excluding O'Neill': this phrase on the title page raises a question that requires an answer at the outset, 'Why?' The explanation is practical: another book in this series, *Eugene O'Neill* by Normand Berlin, treats him. But because no book on American drama of the period can entirely ignore so influential a figure, this one will where appropriate refer to him. 'Excluding O'Neill' has a consequence unrelated to the real reason for his omission. Removal of his shadow from his playwriting colleagues affords a view of them that while not necessarily better is certainly different. They may stand or fall on the basis of their own merits or demerits. This book will discuss both.

1918–45, the dates of the conclusions of this century's two world wars, a phrase I hope the rest of the century does not invalidate, conveniently circumscribes the period when America's first wave of major dramatists came of age. True, Elmer Rice preceded O'Neill with a play on Broadway; but the modernity of Rice's work post-dates the emergence of O'Neill, to whom he like so many stands indebted. True, Arthur Miller's *The Man Who Had All the Luck* opened on Broadway in 1944 and Tennessee Williams' *The Glass Menagerie* did so in 1945; but few would quarrel with the assertions that Miller's important work began three years later with the production of *All My Sons* and that he and Williams represent a newer, post-Second World War wave different from the first. It is equally true that several members of the first wave continued to write plays after 1945. However, the works on which their reputations lie are without exception those written during the period 1918–45: even Thornton Wilder's *The Matchmaker* (1945) is essentially the same play produced in 1938 as *The Merchant of Yonkers*. For this reason, and also because of space limitations, I refer to their post-1945 plays only when such references help to illuminate aspects of their work in general (for instance, Clifford Odets' *The Country Girl*, 1950, dramatises Group Theatre acting techniques that inform his playwriting practices). Unless otherwise indicated, dates are of first productions.

In considering the dramatists of this period, space limitations suggest either a sketchy survey of many writers or a close examination of relatively few. I have chosen the second option. Although any list of important playwrights is debatable, most critics or readers would probably concur with or at least grant me the prerogative of all but one of my selections: Elmer Rice, E. E. Cummings, George S. Kaufman and Moss Hart, Maxwell Anderson, Clifford Odets, Thornton Wilder, Lillian Hellman and William Saroyan. The possible exception is Cummings, whose name and titles I write in conformity with conventional practice and in defiance of his idiosyncratic avoidance of capital letters. Cummings' *Him*, first performed over half a century ago, remains controversial. I include him and *Him* partly because it exemplifies a theatrical genre, surrealism; partly because I greatly admire the play; and partly because a work that creates such diverse critical responses deserves attention and exposure to readers, whom I urge to turn from my account to the play itself and form their own judgments.

Even limiting the subject to eight authors (with Kaufman and Hart as one), space restrictions impose a problem, since between them they wrote about two hundred plays, from a high of over fifty by Rice (his own count) to a low of three by Cummings. To treat all their plays, or all produced between 1918 and 1945 (about sixty less), would prevent scrutiny of works that are more important or representative. Therefore each chapter that examines these dramatists provides an overview of their dramatic and theatrical characteristics, but not always of every play they wrote, which could too easily become mere name-dropping. It will survey their original plays, not translations, and then with one exception concentrate on one play for more intensive study of dramatic and theatrical characteristics. The exception is Elmer Rice, whose two major works are in different dramatic and theatrical styles, expressionism and naturalism. Dramatic and theatrical: the chapters will try to analyse both, for these plays were written for performance on a stage and what is performed is dramatic literature. Analyses of these plays will include their first productions, in some cases revivals as well. Their selection derives from familiarity and interests of theatregoers and readers (on the bases of revivals, books in print and works anthologised), critical interest or consensus, and variety of genre. The plays to receive more attention than others are Rice's *The Adding Machine* and *Street Scene*, Cummings' *Him*, Kaufman and Hart's *You Can't Take It With You*, Anderson's

American Dramatists 1918–1945

Winterset, Odets' *Awake and Sing!*, Wilder's *Our Town*, Hellman's *The Little Foxes*, and Saroyan's *The Time of Your Life*.

As some may have noticed, all but *Him* and *Awake and Sing!* have been turned into films. For three reasons I will where possible refer to them. First, the reader may have seen them at cinema clubs, film societies, revival houses or on television. Second, he or she may be sufficiently familiar with the work of an actor to imagine the actor's rendering of a role. Third, substantive changes in a play's transition from stage to screen can by contrast reveal aspects of the play.

To avoid a proliferation of notes, references that a reader can find with little difficulty (a review of a production, for example) will be unnoted. Because so many dramatists employ three periods, the conventional mark of ellipses, to suggest a pause or a stammer, I place three periods in brackets to indicate ellipses.

For their friendly assistance in helping me to rummage through files of clippings and photographs, it is a pleasure to acknowledge the staff of the Billy Rose Theatre Collection at the New York Public Library at Lincoln Center and of the Theatre Collection of the Museum of the City of New York, particularly Wendy Warnken, Associate Curator. For their help in research, I thank Yukihiro Goto, Nina Hettema and Therese Moore.

1
Watershed Years

History seldom provides tidy dates for the beginning or end of a theatrical period. Sparta's victory over Athens in 404 BC ended the Peloponnesian War and what is now called Old Comedy, which survives in nine of Aristophanes' eleven extant plays; what is now called Middle Comedy supplanted it and survives in the other two. But when did Middle become New? Often, critics regard Henrik Ibsen's *A Doll's House* (1879) – or *A Doll House*, as Rolf Fjelde's frequently performed American translation is called – as the start of modern drama. But one can make a plausible case for Ibsen's *Pillars of Society* (1877) as the first modern play. If impact is a factor, *A Doll's House* has pride of place over *Pillars of Society*. If not, one might go back as many as four decades to cite Georg Büchner's 'modern' *Woyzeck* (1837). And critics disagree on the first expressionistic play, even whether Strindberg or a German wrote it.

For American drama significant to warrant worldwide attention the designation of a starting point is atypically easy. It begins with Eugene O'Neill, who led the way for

American writers to compose plays different from those written before his advent, which occurred on 4 February 1920, when his first full-length play, *Beyond the Horizon*, written in 1918, received a professional production on Broadway. Reviews were quick to perceive, perhaps to overestimate, its value: 'a great play' (*New York Telegram*), 'the play has greatness in it' (*New York Times*). It won the Pulitzer Prize for the best American play of that season – the second time in four years that the prize had been given. On 3 November 1920, only nine months later, O'Neill consolidated his reputation with the off-Broadway production of *The Emperor Jones*, with (at his insistence) a black actor in the leading role. Ecstatic reviews declared O'Neill to be 'the best of American playwrights' (*New York Tribune*), with 'no rival among the American writers for the stage' (*New York Times*). *The Emperor Jones* transferred to Broadway. Thus, 1918–20 form the watershed years of American drama and theatre. O'Neill's fame quickly spread to Europe, whose critics visited America and were just as impressed by his plays as were the Americans. Only 31 years old when *Beyond the Horizon* opened, O'Neill became America's first dramatist of international stature.

Not coincidentally, his composition of the play and its option by a New York producer occurred the same year as the Armistice that ended what was optimistically called the war to end all wars. The war had changed America, which recognised its newer and greater international responsibilities. To many, the familiar clichés were insufficient to interpret a life and a world that seemed different (many others to whom they sufficed found them in films, which during the war years increased in popularity as an entertainment medium). With the ascent of America as a world power came the ascent of New York as an international theatrical power, a city artists visited to display their wares

A REVIEW COPY FROM

Grove Press

DISTRIBUTED BY RANDOM HOUSE, INC.

WE WOULD APPRECIATE RECEIVING TWO
COPIES OF THE REVIEW.

CODE: 039462340
TITLE: AMERICAN DRAMATISTS: 1918-1945
AUTHOR: BERNARD F. DUKORE
PRICE: $7.95
PUB DATE   MAY 10, 1985
           AVAIL. GROVE HARDCOVER $19.50

PLEASE DO NOT RUN YOUR REVIEW BEFORE
PUBLICATION DATE.

and where critics arrived to see the best of the New World's offerings. O'Neill was the right man in the right place at the right time. His example revealed other right men and women.

But what were New York and New York theatre like earlier? For one thing, New York City as we know it – with the areas south, east and northeast of Manhattan joined to it to form a single city – had at the turn of the century existed for only two years. Washington Square's Marble Arch, a Greenwich Village landmark, was a mere 5 years old in 1900 and the Statue of Liberty in New York Harbour 14 years old. Since elevators that made office space on high floors accessible were relatively recent and not widespread (few residential buildings had them), 1900 saw few of the skyscrapers that were to become a prominent feature of New York City. The underground subway was four years into the future. Automobiles moved on New York streets, which nevertheless were dominated by horses that drew carriages, fire engines and street cars. Although the telephone was more reliable, and its use therefore more widespread, in New York than in London, it was still considered a luxury in private homes. New York was a smaller city then in a simpler time than today.

And its drama was simpler. By 1900 New York City was the hub of American theatre, but its plays were naïve and provincial. While other American cities had theatre managers, resident actors and stock companies, New York increasingly became the focus and a play's reception there was the measure of success. With most of the money, it increasingly became the source of productions. Out-of-town meant 'the road', where productions tried out before risking the gauntlet of New York City's reviewers and where productions played if they succeeded in New York. If Gotham, as New York City was called (today it is the Big

Apple), received a play favourably, the producer might organise a second company to perform in Chicago or another large city. After, sometimes during, the New York run, one or more touring companies would take the show on the road, the number depending on the extent of New York success. The road was often a gruelling experience for actors, who might in six nights play in six cities hundreds of miles apart. In the early part of the century, theatre artists were either ununionised or members of ineffective unions. Not until 1919, as a result of a strike, did managers recognise the Actors Equity Association as a collective bargaining agency. Until then, exploitation prevailed: no minimum salary, no rehearsal pay, no bond posted to ensure that an actor would receive pay, dismissal without notice (despite weeks of rehearsal), and the possibility that a play could close and the manager leave the company stranded a thousand or more miles from New York. The Authors League of America, founded in 1912, mainly concerned itself with publication; only when it formed a militant subdivision, the Dramatists Guild, over a dozen years later, did dramatists have an effective bargaining agent.

The popular term for American, particularly Broadway, theatre – Show Biz – is apt. Biz is business, a commercial venture that employs artists for profit. Today's American theatre, which in many ways is more diverse than theatre before O'Neill and which includes private, municipal, state and federal subsidy, is still primarily Show Biz, especially on Broadway; but it lags behind other countries in non-commercial funding. Early in this century, however, American theatre had no non-commercial funding. From the start it was strictly a business enterprise – in contrast to the theatres of almost every other country. If one grasps this factor, all aspects of professional American drama and

4

theatre until O'Neill, and most aspects since, fall into place. However discriminating a producer might be, he could not stay in business long if his plays did not turn profits. Consequently, he presented plays that conformed to audiences' tastes as measured by recent successes and audiences' prejudices as measured by the cries of those whose moral sensitivities had been offended.

Before the watershed years 1918–20, America had no television, not even radio, and while silent films lured audiences from living theatre, talkies were in the future. Theatre was where one went for harmless entertainment with one's wife, adolescent children and maiden aunt. If one wanted intellectual stimulation, challenges to prevalent morality, or probes of life's problems, one went elsewhere. Before these years, the American drama held three things to be sacrosanct: God, who was in his heaven ensuring that all was right with the world, especially the New World; Nation, whose star-spangled banner was a grand flag and after the centennial of 1876 old as well; and Family, with its cottage small by a waterfall, a conception of motherhood only the tiniest distance from divinity, and idyllic children who were all innocence. The theatre of the post-war period did not immediately smash these ideas to smithereens – and film censorship enshrined and embalmed them in the popular consciousness until well after the Second World War – but the watershed years began a process of erosion, led by O'Neill. If God were in his heaven, some believed, then he, she, or it seemed indifferent to human beings. What George M. Cohan, that Yankee Doodle Dandy, called a grand old flag flew over slums and the unemployed. Mother love could suffocate and warp, children behave maliciously. In short, the real world increasingly intruded on the theatrical world of make-believe, though it did not always do so realistically.

This encroachment of the real world stands as contrast to a theatrical world prepared to reject the offerings of O'Neill and his adventurous colleagues. William Winter, the American equivalent of the British Clement Scott, harangued like Scott against the immorality of such dramatists as Ibsen. As late as 1913 Winter said that Ibsen invited audiences to crawl into a sewer with him; that didacticism, as in *A Doll's House*, had nothing to do with drama; and that *Ghosts*, disgusting and loathsome to good taste, had no place in the theatre, which was not a home for sociology or ugliness. American censors threatened verbally frank authors who used such words as 'Hell' and 'God damn', and authors whose frankness avoided them. In 1913 the police stopped a performance of George Scarborough's *The Lure*, set in a brothel. Prostitution is *Mrs. Warren's Profession*, by Bernard Shaw, who sets no scene in a bordello and whose characters utter no obscenity. Nevertheless in 1905 Anthony Comstock, an official of the New York Society for the Suppression of Vice, denounced the play as abominable, unhealthy and as clean as a pig sty; and he was instrumental in inciting the police to close it, charge its producer and actors with disorderly conduct, and haul them before a magistrate, who had the common sense to acquit them (Shaw coined the term 'Comstockery', which stuck). Still, British censorship prevented public production in England for another twenty years. Boston was more censorious than New York and Broadway producers used to try to attract audiences by advertising that a play had been banned in Boston, a phrase that promised a sexual or linguistic thrill.

During these pre-watershed years, professionally produced plays were mostly unsophisticated, sentimental, puerile and hopelessly contrived. To use the argot of the period, they consisted of bunkum and hokum, piffle and twaddle – in other words, they were claptrap, worthless, untrue to life, sentimental, trivial, empty and filled with idle chatter. In such works as *Little Johnny Jones* (1904) and *Forty-Five Minutes from Broadway* (1906), George M. Cohan purveyed catchy music, sentimental comedy and a large dose of flagwaving. Farces were no naughtier than the heroine of Victor Herbert's *Naughty Marietta* (1910) and just as nice, all wholesome fun for the family, as were romances. But musicals, farces and romances were unpretentious confections. Not so plays like *The Great Divide* (1906) by William Vaughn Moody, which suggests barriers between temperaments as well as sections of America, but which is self-consciously literary (it contains, for instance, a reference to Dante by a non-literary character) and has a resolution based on the power of love to overcome all, or those of Edward Sheldon, whose *The Easiest Way* (1909) sets forth a seemingly daring situation about a fallen woman but, in the manner of Dumas *fils'* and Pinero's drama, is conventionally moralistic. Apparently a realist, Clyde Fitch wrote *The City* (1909), superficially about corruption; but it upholds small-town American values and has an innocent woman die to redeem others. Augustus Thomas exploited current ideas or fads in tawdry melodramas: hypnotism in *The Witching Hour* (1907), for example, whose denouement has a would-be victim save himself by hypnotising a man about to shoot him. Such up-to-date gimmickry helped make his trite plays seem more realistic than they were.

More famous as a showman than a dramatist is David Belasco, whose sentimental, hackneyed drama requires no commentary but whose productions do, since he expended much ingenuity to mount empty plays with the utmost realism in lighting and scenery. His sunsets supposedly rivalled nature's. Aware of the clash between twodimensional painted scenery and three-dimensional actors, he substituted three-dimensional reproductions of reality for painted reproductions. He permitted nothing so destructive of illusion as walls flapping when actors touched them. Aiming to reproduce reality with absolute fidelity, he gave painstaking attention to the most minute detail – down to the day of the week printed on a visiting card in *The Governor's Lady* (1912). On some occasions he brought reality itself onstage. For a scene in a shabby boarding house in *The Easiest Way*, he purchased the interior of one of the more dilapidated rooms of such a house – including tarnished and broken gas fixtures, threadbare carpet and faded wallpaper – and placed them on the stage. Belascan realism also embraced what was visible offstage. A Belasco window opened not on to a clear sky but on to a meticulously detailed architectural composition or landscape. Such settings endowed the meretricious pre-O'Neill Broadway drama with the appearance of reality. Also, many who opposed Broadway drama opposed its stagecraft as well.

Before 1900 Paris had its *Théâtre Libre*, Berlin its *Freie Bühne*, London its Independent Theatre, Moscow its Art Theatre, and Dublin its Irish Literary Theatre (precursor of the Abbey). While American theatre personnel knew about them, no American city had anything comparable. Americans were also familiar with Adolphe Appia's and Gordon Craig's ideas on scenic reform: instead of realistic scenery, they advocated the beautiful and the poetic, the simple and the suggestive, the expression of the play's fundamental mood and atmosphere, the symbolic and the three-dimensional. When American art theatres arose early in this century they absorbed both the realism of the *Théâtre Libre* and the anti-realism of Appia and Craig.

Because of the commercial basis of the Broadway

theatre, it is unsurprising that – despite Broadway productions of Ibsen and of Shaw, who was popular in America
before he was in England – the new European drama and
stagecraft first had its major impact in America outside
New York. Throughout America in the new century, art
theatres presented new European plays (plus promising,
usually one-act native works), which they often mounted
with the simplified type of scenery associated with Appia
and Craig: notably the Wisconsin Dramatic Society (1910),
the Plays and Players Club of Philadelphia (1911), the Toy
Theatre of Boston (1912), and the Chicago Little Theatre
(1912). Of these, the last was perhaps the most influential.
Its director, Maurice Browne, and its designer, C.
Raymond Johnson, employed simple, suggestive scenery,
at times screens in the manner of Craig, and they used
lighting for emotional effects, to convey the mood of the
play, not to recreate a sunrise. One reason the Chicago
Little Theatre was influential is that Browne made its
presence felt – partly by example, partly by writing about its
productions and his ideas, thus reaching an audience
beyond Chicago. A number of those who founded the
Washington Square Players and the Provincetown Players,
to be discussed shortly, were familiar with Browne's work –
some knew him personally – and they acknowledged their
indebtedness to him.

Outside New York, universities began to offer courses in
playwriting, of which the best known is George Pierce
Baker's, begun at Harvard in 1913. Although he taught a
method of working to O'Neill, his most famous student, his
chief contributions, according to O'Neill, were encour-
agement and inspiration. He made his students feel that it
was possible to write plays of imagination, originality and
integrity in America.

New York itself was not immune to European influences. In 1912 Max Reinhardt brought *Sumurun* to Broadway, affording New York theatregoers the opportunity to see an example of stagecraft influenced by Appia and Craig. Three years later Granville Barker produced a double bill of Shaw's *Androcles and the Lion* and Anatole France's *The Man Who Married a Dumb Wife*. For the latter he employed the American designer Robert Edmond Jones, soon to be associated with O'Neill and the Provincetown Players, to provide settings, which he did in the manner of what was then called the New Stagecraft, influenced by Craig. That year D. W. Griffiths' film *The Birth of a Nation* opened, confirming what to many needed no confirmation by this time, that the cinema's realism was better than that of the stage. The way was open to proponents of the New Stagecraft. Assisted by the 1917 New York performances of Jacques Copeau's Vieux Colombier troupe, which used simplified scenery, the newer scene designers were in the ascendant.

While Europe was at war, Greenwich Village, a picturesque section of New York City south of 14th Street and west of Broadway, increased in reputation as a gathering place of artistic, social and political radicals. It was America's Left Bank, a Bohemian enclave whose residents spurned middle-class values, including those connected with the drama. Two new groups were associated with it, the Washington Square Players and the Provincetown Players. Two major American designers, each a proponent of the New Stagecraft, joined them: Lee Simonson the former, Robert Edmond Jones the latter.

Although the name Washington Square Players, founded in 1914, indicates its locus as the Village, where most of its founders lived, the group rejected Village sites as too small for a theatre. Instead, it rented the Bandbox Theatre on 57th Street off Third Avenue, closer to the

Broadway area. In June 1916 it moved to the Comedy Theatre on West 38th Street, owned by the Shubert Brothers, Broadway producers. Among its founders were Lawrence Langner, Philip Moeller, Helen Westley and Edward Goodman. They produced European plays by Maeterlinck, Shaw, Wedekind, Chekhov and Strindberg; also new American plays, including the one-act *Moondown* by John Reed (later to write *Ten Days That Shook the World*, now a personage familiar as the Warren Beatty character in the film *Reds*). After May 1918 the Washington Square Players dissolved, to re-emerge in December as the Theatre Guild, whose first production of an important American play was on 18 March 1923, Elmer Rice's *The Adding Machine*.

In the summer of 1915 a group at Provincetown, Massachusetts, led by George Cram (Jig) Cook and Susan Glaspell, both of whom had been active with the Washington Square Players, organised a theatre group to present informally two one-act plays, Glaspell's and Cook's *Suppressed Desires* and Neith Boyce's *Constancy*, in the parlour of a private home. For a second performance they transformed an old fish wharf on a pier into a theatre, which they used again in the summer of 1916. Their plays, all new and by Americans, included *Freedom* by Reed and *The Game* by Louise Bryant (Diane Keaton in *Reds*). Their second summer helped to change the American theatre. Some of the ways of such groups resemble, before the fact, Mickey Rooney–Judy Garland musicals wherein one says, 'I've got an idea: let's put on a play!' and assisted by the other both play and production materialise. In summer 1916, according to an often-told story, O'Neill was in Provincetown with his sexagenarian friend Terry Carlin (years later, the model for Larry Slade in *The Iceman Cometh*). Glaspell met Carlin and asked if he had a play for

11

her group to read. Carlin replied that he was a talker not a writer, but his young friend wrote plays. She invited O'Neill to read one that evening. He gave her his one-act sea play *Bound East for Cardiff*. Too shy to read it himself, he waited in the dining room while others read. By the end of the reading they were aware of the treasure dropped in their midst and of their purpose. On 28 July 1916, in that converted fish house, an O'Neill play, an apprentice piece but nonetheless important, was first performed. The summer over, the group continued their activities in Greenwich Village. There they converted a stable on Macdougal Street, just steps away from Washington Square, into a theatre (ironically, the Washington Square Players had turned it down as too small) where they presented plays by O'Neill and others. They called themselves the Provincetown Players and the Village theatre became known as the Provincetown Playhouse (from experience in the 1950s I assure readers that the auditorium is small and the stage and backstage areas so cramped as to require an adjective that conveys less sophistication than 'primitive').

The Washington Square Players and the Provincetown Players, Simonson and Jones, the art theatres and the Broadway imports – more than these paved the way for O'Neill's emergence on Broadway. Sometimes literally, the older generation passed away while the newer knocked at the door. Fitch died in 1909, Moody in 1910, Comstock in 1915, Winter in 1917. Such old-guard dramatists as Belasco, Cohan and Thomas wrote with decreasing regularity and effectiveness. *The Theatre*, a magazine associated with the commercial theatre, found a competitor in Sheldon Cheney's *Theatre Arts Magazine*, which in its first issue (1916) opposed theatrical businessmen and true to its name allied itself with artists. Appropriately, it began not in New York, America's commercial theatre centre, but in

Detroit, where that year Sam Hume, influenced by the New Stagecraft, designed scenery for the Detroit Arts and Crafts Theatre. Two years later, when O'Neill wrote *Beyond the Horizon, Theatre Arts* lost local support by praising German theatre. It moved to New York, where conditions had become favourable for it and other new magazines, such as the irreverent *Smart Set*, edited by H. L. Mencken. As O'Neill knew, his plays were not the type of writing printed in *The Smart Set*, but he valued Mencken's opinion and sent him three one-acters, which Mencken admired and showed to his drama critic, George Jean Nathan, who concurred. To O'Neill's surprise, *The Smart Set* published them in 1917 and 1918.

Nathan, one of the newer critics, directed outrageous broadsides at the Broadway theatre, for example: 'It is frequently recommended by the more droll among our dramatic reviewers that audiences, in order to enjoy this or that Broadway play, ought, before they enter the theatre, check their brains in the coat-room. Say what you will against the idea, you must yet admit its thorough practicability. There would still be lots of room left for the coats.'[1] Clayton Hamilton lamented that the fault of most dramatists 'is not – to use Hamlet's phrase – that they "imitate humanity so abominably": it is, rather, that they do not imitate humanity at all. Most of our playwrights [. . .] imitate each other.'[2] He called the American theatre so insular that 'there are certain first nights in New York when, if you should blow up the building with a bomb, you would kill off nearly everybody in America who knows how to write a play'. New York drama reflects not the world of America, not even the world of New York, but the world of Times Square, with the language of Times Square, which is unlike language anywhere else in America.[3]

None of these developments fully explains O'Neill's

success. I agree with Horst Frenz, who contends that since conditions on Broadway 'were restrictive and detrimental to the development of dramatic art' and so rooted in the marketplace tradition, two solutions were possible.

One was to change or eliminate the commercial basis of the serious theatre by means of subvention – something that has never been achieved or even attempted in a radical way. The other was the kind of breakthrough that only a dramatist whose work combined literary quality with wide audience appeal could bring about. Eugene O'Neill was this dramatist, and the breakthrough that he initiated was consolidated later by others of his stature. Nevertheless, fundamental conditions of existence in the American commercial theatre remained unchanged.[4]

What occurred involves the enthusiasm of a persuasive critic, an actor's desire to play a role (still the reason many plays are produced on Broadway and the West End), and luck. George Jean Nathan's enthusiasm for O'Neill brought *Beyond the Horizon* to the attention of Broadway producer John D. Williams, who optioned it in 1918. But it is easier to get a play optioned than produced. Perhaps second thoughts urged caution, for Williams let the play languish almost two years. Then the actor Richard Bennett (readers may have seen him in Orson Welles' film *The Magnificent Ambersons*), who was starring in Williams' production of Elmer Rice's *For the Defense*, happened to see O'Neill's manuscript in Williams' office. The 47-year-old actor determined to play the 23-year-old protagonist. He persuaded Williams to produce the play on the cheap for a series of matinees with actors mainly recruited from the cast of *For the Defence*. The matinees were so successful that *Beyond the Horizon* went into an evening run and *For the Defense* has been virtually forgotten – appropriately, according to Rice, who claims its only virtue is that it indirectly launched 'the brilliant career of the most gifted dramatist America has yet produced', O'Neill.[5]

Beyond the Horizon startled its contemporaries. One reason was its subject, which was shocking and sensational to 1920 theatregoers. Another was its unhappy ending, also unconventional then. O'Neill's characters seemed taken from life, not from other plays, and their language reflected a world beyond Times Square. Also, Americans were ripe for it. Rejection of Victorian conventions and use of realistic language were occurring in fiction: Sherwood Anderson's *Winesburg, Ohio* appeared in 1919, Sinclair Lewis's *Main Street* and F. Scott Fitzgerald's *This Side of Paradise* in 1920. *Beyond the Horizon* signalled a change of taste. The more astute producers recognised the signal and sought works that would not seem old-fashioned in comparison.

In addition, O'Neill heralded the arrival of art in the marketplace. When he requested Baker's permission to attend his playwriting class he told the professor he wanted to become an artist and failing that would rather become nothing. Then, art was not a goal at which the commercial theatre aimed. Art was for small theatres in Europe or the American hinterlands, not Broadway, where a great deal of money was at stake. When Broadway producers heard the word 'art' they did not reach for their revolvers; instead, they repocketed their chequebooks. To some extent O'Neill made it possible for the American theatrical marketplace to accommodate drama that aimed at artistry; before him it was virtually impossible. The principles of commerce remained, but the shrewder businessmen realised that art was not anathema to the paying public. The Show Biz merchants became readier to examine what an idealistic dramatist had to offer. O'Neill helped to make art more acceptable in Broadway's commodity theatre.

2
Elmer Rice

In April 1959, *Theatre Arts* had an article on Elmer Rice entitled 'Playwriting's Old Pro', an allusion to his forty-five years as a dramatist. He is indeed a thorough professional. A salesperson sells wares, a ditchdigger digs ditches, a telephone operator answers phone calls, a writer writes: each putting in his day at store, road, switchboard, desk. Rice's autobiography, *Minority Report*, quantifies his career as a pro: 'some fifty full-length plays (about twenty of them unproduced); four novels, three of which have been published; a book about the theatre; an indeterminate number of short stories, one-act plays, articles, book reviews, motion pictures, radio and television scripts; and the present volume.'

His debut as a professional dramatist was in 1914 when *On Trial* succeeded first on Broadway, then nationally and internationally on stage and screen. On opening night he was one month shy of his twenty-second birthday. For half a century he put in his day. At lucky times inspiration descended. One night he was trying to concentrate on a play when suddenly a new work 'flashed into my mind': plot, events, characters, some dialogue, and the title, *The Adding Machine*, which he claims to have written compulsively and in a trancelike condition in seventeen days. Such occasions are rare. The pro searches for ideas. In 1924, observing the modern mechanised society that crushes human beings, he composed *The Subway*, whose heroine is run over by a train. His observations in Europe bore fruit in *The Left Bank* (1931), about American expatriates in Paris on the left bank of the Seine. In 1945 dreams and psychology were in the public consciousness. That year came Alfred Hitchcock's *Spellbound*, with dream sequences designed by Salvador Dali, and Rice's *Dream Girl*, an amiable confection whose heroine's life and daydreams reveal her psychology. International events affect his work. In 1915, before America entered the First World War, he wrote an anti-war play, *The Iron Cross*. Inspired by the rigged trials in which the Nazis found communists guilty of setting fire to the Reichstag (they themselves did it), he wrote *Judgment Day* (1934), set in an unnamed Balkan country, with characters corresponding to Hitler, Goering and others. In *Flight to the West* (1940) refugees from the Nazis flee Europe and American liberal pacifists realise they must take arms to defend democratic values. The pro is a craftsman. 'The interweaving of incident and the gradual clearing up of the seemingly inexplicable had the fascination of a chess problem', he says, adding, 'I enjoy setting myself puzzles.' When he could not devise one himself, he accepted assignments to dramatise novels and to collaborate with others.

Rice takes pride in his technical skills. His first full-length play, *On Trial*, contains, for the first time in the theatre, flashbacks, and with a twist: dramatising what a witness in court would convey orally, each flashback takes place

earlier than the previous one. But he goes further. 'Just as I
entered my home the telephone in the library rang', says
the victim's wife at the end of the Prologue, whereupon the
first act begins with the phone ringing in an empty room,
which she enters. One scene ends with a child testifying that
on a particular day she was practising her piano lesson; the
new scene begins with the sound of an offstage piano.
Unfortunately, Rice does not consistently provide such
connectives. An otherwise standard courtroom drama, *On
Trial* focuses on a murder apparently committed when the
dead man discovered a robbery in progress, yet the killing
turns out to be a crime of passion and someone else steals
the money. Trite touches pepper the drama, including the
testimony of a darling 8-year-old girl who does well at
classes, regularly attends Sunday School, loves her parents,
and bursts into tears, thereby triggering an emotional
outburst from her father, the defendant.

Like *On Trial, Cock Robin*, written in 1927 with Philip
Barry, is a whodunit, though it is not set in a courtroom.
Alerting audiences to its genre, the title recalls the children's rhyme 'Who Killed Cock Robin?' and the victim is
named Hancock Robinson, nicknamed Robin. The play
follows the conventions of whodunits: a murder, an inves-
tigation, guilt pointed at almost everyone. Because of
Rice's craftsmanship, the central gimmick is probably his:
Cock Robin shows part of a play-within-a-play several
times from different viewpoints. In Act I actors rehearse an
eighteenth-century play (invented by Rice and Barry) in
which the character played by Robin is killed. Act II shows
the same scene in performance, from reverse, its audience
upstage. Here the murder is real. In Act III, which has the
same perspective as Act II, the scene is re-enacted so that
the character who saw it from the auditorium can refresh
her memory. Cleverness underlies cleverness. At the end of

19

Act I the inner play's director tells the actors (and us) that if one plays a murder scene before several hundred people and asks them to record what they saw the result would be several hundred different stories. Therefore, he advises, if anyone wants to kill the author or director, do so 'with five hundred witnesses – the chances are you'll get away with it!' This occurs with us as witnesses, but the killer does not get away with it.

Counsellor-at-Law (1931) contains the hustle and bustle of law offices; it abounds in colourful yet unobtrusive details of law and lawyers (including a young clerk who for thrills reads law cases about rape) and of different types of New Yorkers from recent immigrants to people with old wealth. It offers a fine characterisation of its protagonist, George Simon, who is as proud of his lower-class origins as of his rise from them, who befriends poor clients gratis and extracts as much money as he can from rich clients and adversaries. Its slender plots involve his futile efforts to maintain his marriage to a socialite who dazzles him until he perceives her selfishness and infidelity, in contrast to his secretary's dedication, and his successful efforts to avoid disbarment, based on charges by a socially prominent WASP member of the Bar Association whom he bettered several times. As the Jewish-American Simon tells his Italian-American partner, reflecting the prejudices of the day, 'He's out after *our* scalps, isn't he? and why? Because we came from the streets and our parents talk with an accent.' Several factors save these stories from triteness. Apart from professionally colourful details, characterisation and social background is the Chekhovian technique of keeping the climactic scene between Simon and his legal antagonist offstage. Despite the play's melodramatic basis, and one scene with Simon about to jump from a window, Rice focuses on character and profession. By understating what is conventional and emphasising the fresh characters and ambience, he creates a striking play.

In *We, the People* (1933) he employs his craft on a multi-scenic panorama of social malaise during the Depression. More than fifty characters span a wide spectrum, including industrial worker, foreman, political activist, medical student, university professor, senator, judge and industrialist. The play interweaves such issues as massive firings of workers, large protest meetings, anti-semitism in higher education, and police brutality. Although Rice's capitalists and their allies tend to be villainous, his workers are not invariably noble. This liberal play has two prominent virtues: its demonstration of 'the economic links between the middle and the lower class' and its treatment of race relations. In contrast to most labour plays about race, which have white and black join in brotherhood against capitalists, Rice's demonstrates that 'the tensions of urban poverty and unemployment that whites and blacks share are more likely to aggravate racial animosities than ease them.'[1]

The charming *Two on an Island* (1940) is 'about' New York City more than anything else. Its wisp of a plot suffices to present a kaleidoscopic view of the titular island, Manhattan. Throughout, the stories of a young man and woman interweave. In the first scene they arrive in Manhattan, take cabs to different destinations, and during the first two acts their paths cross but do not converge. In Act III they meet, live together, marry, and she becomes pregnant. Rice handles places and character types skilfully, juxtaposing different New York areas and the people in them, including out-of-town visitors. In several scenes, such as a subway and a restaurant, groups of people speak within each group but not to people in other groups. Their dialogue, varied to conform to classes and places of origin,

21

ebbs and flows, one group becoming audible as the others fade.

In many instances Rice's dialogue is vivid. For a pre-Armistice play *The Iron Cross*, for the most part trite, is daringly anti-religious (perhaps one reason it was not professionally produced): 'A bloody war breaks out, kills millions of people, makes millions of others suffer and you say it's the work of God. A brute of a Cossack comes along and ravishes you, makes you the mother of a child that will be a source of sorrow all its life, and you comfort yourself by saying it's God's punishment for your sins! What sins did you ever commit I'd like to know!' To give audiences a sense of the profession, *Counsellor-at-Law* cunningly explains legal jargon to outsiders. Simon dictates a letter:

I am returning herewith your money order for fifty dollars, as I was actuated – No, strike that out: she won't understand it. As I handled your daughter's case only because of our old friendship and because of my interest in you and your family. I am sorry it was impossible [. . .] to obtain a larger settlement, but inasmuch as there was no liability on the part of the defendant – No, strike that out. But owing to the fact that the trucking company was to blame, I could not do better.

Rice adapts language to character, for instance: 'The dirty little tightwad. Tryin' to jew me down a few thousand dollars after all the pearls and Rolls-Royces he was goin' to buy me'; 'You don't hoid? He's already dead six years. [. . .] He's got in de stomach a cancer'; 'Oh, you just came in, did you? Well, you can just get out again. I don't want to see your mug around here.' The first speaker is a tart and the infinitive verb is slang, not anti-semitism (she addresses

22

Simon, a Jew); the second is a Jewish immigrant; the third is Simon, who combines balanced antitheses with slang that reveals lower-class origins. *Two on an Island* hits precisely the right notes, catching local colour, comedy, appropriate clichés, and pronunciation of a tour guide who, referring to the Heinz company's well-advertised '57 varieties' of condiments, regales tourists with statistics and pseudo-statistics about New York:

> Now, I'd just like to point out that every day in the year, including Sundays and legal holidays, New York has a daily average of one hundred and fifteen thousand visitors, a human influx equal in size to the entire population of Spokane, Washington, or Fort Wayne, Indiana. The world's greatest city, seven million six hundred thousand people, fifty-seven nationalities, fifty-seven varieties in the Heinz League of Nations, twenty-one thousand policemen, one hundred and thirty-seven hospitals, two hundred and ninety-seven thousand dogs, five hundred thousand cats, more or less, six hundred and thirty-eight churches, fifteen thousand taxicabs. Half the life of the city is spent ducking the taxicab drivers.

When they approach Washington Square he introduces 'Green Witch Village', where 'women go hatless and men wear long hair. (*Suddenly pointing*) There's one right there on the corner! (*Passengers all turn to look.*)'. Rice captures the clichés of out-of-towners – 'the way I figure it, it's a wonderful town to visit but I wouldn't live here if you gave me the place' – and the wisecracking lingo of the day, as in this interview between an actress and a producer: 'Do you want to know what I've done?' 'No. But tell me anyhow.' 'Well, to begin at the very beginning, I've been mad about the stage ever since I was about five –' 'Let's get down to modern times. I'm catching a midnight train.'

Far be it from me to imply that Rice's dialogue is invariably good. In *On Trial* Mrs Trask *'suspiciously'* asks her husband's male secretary the identity of a woman. When he disclaims knowledge, she retorts, 'I suppose my husband doesn't take his secretary into his confidence to that extent, although he doesn't make any great attempt to keep things secret. He hasn't even a sense of shame.' As if in confession of such clumsy exposition, Rice has her explain, 'I don't ordinarily discuss these things; but even my endurance has its limits.' *The Iron Cross* abounds in such stilted language as 'You've dishonoured me – defiled my home!' *Judgment Day* has numerous clichés, for instance:

PARVAN: We have learned our lesson. In the future we shall know how to deal with our enemies.
GEORGE: Have you enough battalions for that?
JUDGE TSANKOV: (*striking the table*). Enough of these treasonable utterances!

In *American Landscape* (1938) an old American family prevents Nazis from acquiring its property. The patriarch tritely and pretentiously declaims:

But in you, Connie, in you, Fran, the blood of the Dale family still flows, fused with strange new blood into strong and honest strains. That is the chemistry of America. These few belongings that I knew and loved are yours now. Use them wisely and use them well. In material things, your heritage is a meagre one: an old house, a few acres, a little workshop. But man does not live by bread alone. And ever and above my worldly

24

goods, I leave you a tradition that is rich and deep and
alive: a tradition of freedom and of the common rights of
humanity. It's a priceless inheritance. Cherish it! Cherish
it! And be prepared to defend it.

Staleness subverts sincerity. In *A New Life* (1943) imagery
and cliché do not slyly mock the speaker as in *Two on an
Island*. Instead, they resemble the numbingly forced
dialogue of Hollywood 'B' films: 'Don't you know who that
umbrella-merchant is? He's big boss of Consolidated
Steel.' 'What do you mean: umbrella-merchant?' 'Munich!
Appeasement! He was one of the original let's-do-
business-with-Hitler boys until a flock of war contracts
turned him into a super-duper patriot.' The topical
references that once helped *Dream Girl* to succeed now
help to date it: a radio advisor on personal problems,
parodying the popular Mr Anthony, interrupts the day-
dreamer to admonish her to use initials rather than real
names and to avoid such unacceptable words as 'incestu-
ous'; the novel *Forever Amber* (mild today, then considered racy) is thinly disguised as *Always Opal*; and
allusions include such journalists as John Kieran and
Westbrook Pegler.

To different degrees, theatricality marks virtually all
Rice's plays, heralded by the flashbacks of his first. At the
start of *Cock Robin* actors rehearse in eighteenth-century
costumes and when interrupted remove their wigs and light
cigarettes (Rice and Barry knew their Pirandello: titled *The
Living Mask*, his *Henry IV*, which employs these devices,
had opened in New York five years earlier). The two
settings of *Counsellor-at-Law* suggest a microcosm of New
York and by extension America: one has a window with a
panoramic view of lower Manhattan, the other a window
showing Manhattan buildings, beyond them the Hudson

River, and still further the New Jersey shore. *Judgment Day* contains such melodramatic 'big curtains' as an attempted suicide, a bomb explosion, and the assassination of the Hitler figure followed by the assassin's suicide. *Two on an Island* begins with two cut-out taxicabs facing the audience, each individualised: the independent-owner cab is dingy and decrepit, the cab that belongs to a large fleet bright and shiny. As the cabbies mime driving, they comment on the locales and complain to and about other drivers. One scene has a sightseeing bus cut diagonally to show the tour guide and passengers. Another set is a longitudinal section of a subway car, with passengers who mime the jerky ride. After a man propositions the heroine of *Dream Girl* she daydreams she is a prostitute: with cheap red coat, ratty fur collar, gaudy hat on a tousled blond wig, and a lamp post beside her.

'The Adding Machine'

In 1923 old-fashioned reviewers found *The Adding Machine* shocking. While the *New York Times* judged it 'the best' example of theatrical expressionism to play in New York, it called one scene 'gratuitously vulgar', an allusion to a prostitute's suggestion that she and her client engage in sex on the grave of the protagonist, who informed on her activities to the police. The *New York Commercial* thought the play would 'inevitably corrode the moral fibre'. Considered old-guard by some, *Theatre* raved: if the play had come from Prague, it 'would excite the townsfolk to prayer and feasting. [. . .] But being the work of an American, and an American, incidentally, not of the esoteric order, we can expect a merely mild critical reception and a patronizing attitude of "Not so bad, not so

26

bad", all of which is depressing but inevitable.' *Theatre* misjudged the response. In fact, the play's box-office success surprised everyone.

I have found no clearer summary of the work than the author's:

> It was the case history of one of the slave souls who are both the raw material and the product of a mechanised society. In eight scenes it told the story of Mr. Zero, a white-collar worker tied to a monotonous job and a shrewish wife. Replaced by a machine, he murders his boss in an access of resentment and panic, and he is condemned to die by a jury of his peers. His fears and frustrations make him reject an eternity of happiness and self-expression; he returns to earth to begin another treadmill existence, sustained only by the mirage of hope.

The Adding Machine may be the first American play to dramatise human beings nonentitised by mechanised society. Its protest is moral, not social, universal and never strident. It accuses not capitalism but modern industrialism, which degrades human beings in the Soviet Union as much as in the United States. Zero is what was called a 'white-collar slave', individually as insignificant as his name but symbolically significant in that he represents millions of maleducated, credulous drudges easily manipulated by those in power. Middle-class morality has so warped him that he is incapable of enjoying non-marital sex in the Elysian Fields. In a letter printed in *The World* (29 March 1923) Rice calls Zero's psychology that of a slave. Anticipating Peter Barnes' *The Bewitched* by fifty-one years, he adds, 'the one thing that the slave hates and fears beyond all things is liberty. For the slave senses unconsciously that authority means not only exemption from thought, but security. The power which enslaves him protects him as well.' For people like Zero, death is not a conclusion. He is one of those who wind up for recycling in the ladle of Ibsen's Button Moulder, in *Peer Gynt*, which Rice had read. With each new incarnation Zero worsens. As a monkey he kowtowed to larger or smarter monkeys, but at least he was healthy. Later, kings and bosses kicked him and his iron collar in a Roman galley was eventually replaced by his white collar in a dingy office. In his next incarnation, 'the final triumph of the evolutionary process', he will operate a 'super-hyper-adding machine' by toe. Rice blames a cosmic 'rotten system'.

If the cosmos is rotten and the mark of the slave imprinted on Zero's soul from the start, as the last scene states, why not resign ourselves to the status quo? Is not sympathy for the Zeroes of the world irrelevant? Rice implies negative answers. Thunder and lightning intimidate a potentially rebellious Zero when he wants to quit, but we need not be intimidated by special effects. Rice offers no specific remedies. Instead, he challenges the spectators, who may not respond as Zero does – unless they resemble him.

Although *The Adding Machine* is expressionistic, Rice has denied the influence of expressionism, claiming that he read no German expressionist plays until after he had written it. Nevertheless, New York saw O'Neill's *Emperor Jones* in 1920, his *Hairy Ape* and Georg Kaiser's *From Morn to Midnight* in 1922 – all expressionistic. It is inconceivable that Rice was unaware of O'Neill's plays and he read reviews of Kaiser's. In a memorandum he wrote during 1923 rehearsals, he explicitly discusses *The Adding Machine* as an 'expressionistic play'. Furthermore, at a private screening in Hollywood in 1920, he saw the expressionistic German film *The Cabinet of Dr. Caligari* and though admittedly 'greatly impressed' by it says he did not have it consciously in mind when he wrote his play.[2] The reason for his denials is his desire to differentiate *The Adding Machine*, as a work of creative imagination, from his craftsmanlike plays. As he explains, 'You don't start off with a theory, you know. You have something to say and the subject matter compels the form. You don't begin with a form and then pour something into it, unless you're writing a purely mechanical thing as I did with [. . .] *On Trial*'.[3]

Rice calls expressionism an attempt 'not so much to depict events faithfully as to convey to the spectator what seems to [the author] to be their inner significance. To achieve this end the dramatist often finds it expedient to depart entirely from objective reality and to employ symbols, condensations and a dozen devices which, to the conservative, must seem arbitrarily fantastic.' Expressionism departs from surface realism to convey a different type of reality. As its name implies, such a play externally *expresses* the abstract or what Rice's memorandum calls the 'inner life'. Its means include distillation (to an essence, be it character, feeling, mood, or idea), amplification (of that distilled essence, examined in various aspects), and consequently distortion of surface reality. As the expressionist painter and playwright Wassily Kandinsky says, 'The quantitative reduction of the abstract is related to its qualitative intensification'.[4] Characters may be fragmented or reduced to type. Time may be telescoped or extended. In whole or in part, scenery and lighting may abandon realism to express mood, feeling or idea. Settings might depict the essence of environment; and if they include realistic elements they highlight or give them a non-realistic context. Expressionistic dialogue includes

29

clipped, telegraphic fragments of sentences, soliloquies, choral or group chants or speech, and both poetry and prose.

Scene 2 of *The Adding Machine* externally represents the inner (thoughts) and the abstract (work as numbing routine). As Daisy reads figures, Zero enters them in a ledger: 'Three ninety-eight. Forty-two cents. A dollar fifty. A dollar fifty. A dollar twenty-five. Two dollars.' Repetitions of 'A dollar' contribute to the sense of monotonous existence. Each speaks his thoughts while the other without looking up quietly intones figures. 'Gee, I'd like to make a date with her', says Zero. 'You could look a long time before you'd find a sensible, refined girl like me', says Daisy. Less evident on the page than in performance is the constant intonation of figures, which denies any life-affirming thoughts the characters may express and which reveals such thoughts to be unfulfillable daydreams of human automata.

Expressionistically, Rice shows Zero tried by a jury of his peers – ciphers like him – in an unrealistic but unmistakable courtroom:

Three bare white walls without door or windows except for a single door in the right wall. At the right is a jury box in which are seated MESSRS. ONE, TWO, THREE, FOUR, FIVE, *and* SIX *and their respective wives. On either side of the jury box stands a uniformed officer. Opposite the jury box is a long, bare oak table piled high with law books. Behind the books* ZERO *is seated, his face buried in his hands. There is no other furniture in the room.*

For the 1923 Theatre Guild production Lee Simonson eliminated the law books and table. Instead, the vertical lines of the railing around the dock, the judge's overly high desk and the windows were at sharp angles and like justice distorted; to express the judge's impassiveness, Simonson gave him a mask.

Through skilful juxtapositions, which give the impression of free association, of period slang ('Nix'), mispronunciation ('Young Kipper' for 'Yom Kippur'), New York accent ('empire' for 'umpire'), loss of control ('Twenty-five years. Never missed a day, and never more'n five minutes late. Look at my time card if you don't believe me. Eight twenty-seven, eight thirty, eight twenty-nine, eight twenty-seven, eight thirty-two. Eight an' thirty-two's forty an' – Goddam them figures!'), religious and racial prejudice ('The dirty sheenies', 'The dirty Nigger!'), the urge for violence bred by repression ('I'd like to been there, with a gat in each hand, pumpin' him full of lead'), and cowardice ('when I seen the cop comin' up the aisle, I beat it'), Rice turns realistic speech into expressionism, conveying the frenzied mind of an inarticulate man. Theatrically, he reveals the harshly mechanical and regimented system: in unison, jurors rise, shout 'GUILTY!', turn and walk out of the court.

In the final scene Rice has Zero sit by an adding machine, mechanically pressing its keys and pulling its lever. A strip of white papertape flows from it. *'It covers the floor and the furniture, it climbs the walls and chokes the doorways'.* Lee Simonson provided an effective alternative. A gigantic adding machine dominated the stage. Its keys were as large as barstools and required much effort for Zero to move from one to another and to press them down. However, the set need not be elaborate. In a professional workshop production directed by Warren Berlinger in New York in 1959, ordinary chairs became the keys of an otherwise imaginary adding machine.

The scene wherein Zero kills his boss conveys the

31

turmoil of Zero's mind and suggests the murder without showing it. Expecting a reward for twenty-five years of work without a day's absence, Zero is dazed when the Boss – who does not know his name – calmly but firmly tells him that as he will be replaced by an adding machine he is fired. Rice expresses Zero's growing frenzy: '*Soft music is heard – the sound of the mechanical player of a distant merry-go-round. The part of the floor upon which the desks and stools are standing begins to revolve very slowly*.' As the Boss continues, '*The music becomes gradually louder and the revolutions more rapid*'. With Zero in a literal whirl, the Boss, '*barely making himself heard above the increasing volume of sound*', telegraphically speaks only what enters Zero's consciousness: 'I'm sorry – no other alternative – greatly regret – old employee – efficiency – economy – business – *business* – BUSINESS –' until the music drowns his voice. The Platform revolves rapidly. The men face each other – '*motionless save for the* BOSS'*s jaws, which open and close incessantly. But the words are inaudible*.' To the swelling music Rice adds '*every offstage effect of the theatre: the wind, the waves, the galloping horses, the locomotive whistle, the sleigh bells, the automobile siren, the glass-crash, New Year's Eve, Election Night, Armistice Day, and Mardi Gras*.' Augmenting this effect, Simonson projected a jumble of rotating numbers of a screen. Sound, movement and projection culminate in a thunderclap, followed by an instantaneous flash of red – two flashes in the Guild's production – before the stage is suddenly darkened. Whether one interprets the red flash(es) as blood or as Zero's 'seeing red' (becoming enraged, losing his self-control), and reviewers have done both, it is clear that a murder occurs.

Rice portrays the lives of white-collar workers and their wives as dull and uniform, their concerns trivial, their speech clichés. Messrs Zero, One through Six, and their wives – whose names express cipherdom – wear identical suits or dresses, though the dresses have different colours and each person wears a differently coloured wig. The Ones through Sixes file into the Zeroes' home in a double column. Mrs Zero takes each woman's hand and: 'How de do, Mrs. One.' 'How de do, Mrs. Zero.' Zero silently shakes each man's hand. They sit, segregated by sex. Their party conversation begins with clichés, such as 'Y' can't always go by the papers' and 'Yeh, it's all the way you look at it'. Gradually, their frustrations emerge as rage against those different from them in nationality, religion and race. Beginning as clichés ('Too damn many strikes', 'They ought to be run outa the country', 'America for the Americans is what I say!'), they explode into unrealistic choral speech ('That's it! Damn foreigners! Damn dagoes! Damn Catholics! Damn sheenies! Damn niggers! Jail 'em! Shoot 'em! Hang 'em! Lynch 'em! Burn 'em!') and a song with ironic lyrics ('My country 'tis of thee,/Sweet land of liberty!').

The contrast between the characters whose names are ciphers and Daisy Diana Dorothea Devore is more apparent than actual, since her proliferation of names has the effect of nullifying an individualised identity. Moreover, her three given names point, in typical expressionist fashion, to a single trait, virginity: the flower whose petals close at night, the goddess associated with chastity, and the virgin saint mocked by a pagan as the bride only of the dead Jesus; her surname, derived from Deborah, may ironically allude to the Hebrew prophetess who urged, invoking God's will, that the Israelites free themselves from the yoke of the Canaanites (Miss Devore, in the Elysian Fields scene, unsuccessfully urges Zero to free himself from the manacles of middle-class morality). Also named for a single

33

characteristic is the prostitute Judy O'Grady (as Kipling points out, she and the colonel's lady are sisters under the skin).

The opening speech, a three-page monologue by Mrs Zero, reproduces what Rice calls 'authentic speech':

> I'm gettin' sick o' them Westerns. All of them cowboys ridin' around an' foolin' with them ropes. I don't care nothin' about that. I'm sick of 'em. I don't see why they don't have more of them stories like *For Love's Sweet Sake*. I like them sweet little love stories. They're nice an' wholesome. Mrs. Twelve was sayin' to me only yesterday, 'Mrs. Zero', says she, 'what I like is one of them wholesome stories, with just a sweet, simple little love story.' 'You're right, Mrs. Twelve', I says. 'That's what I like too.' They're showin' too many Westerns at the Rosebud.

Although the actress speaks realistically, the characters' names and the repetitions help to undermine the effect of realism, to place the dialogue under a microscope, as it were, and to provide a non-realistic context – as does the silence of Zero, whose head and shoulders are visible while he lies in bed. In setting too, authenticity has an unrealistic context: *an "installment plan" bed, dresser, and chairs'*, an ugly electric light fixture with a naked lamp, but the walls are *'covered with columns of figures'*. Rice also plunges the audience into the silent Zero's world of numbers by Mrs Zero's references to Mrs Twelve, Mrs Nine, a movie star's two marriages, hours of day, and (eight times) the number of years he has been a bookkeeper. Her nagging shows both to be nonentities and victims.

Much of the play is funny. Even a cemetery scene ends on a comic note. A grave opens and a head appears, complaining: 'Can't you shut up and let a guy sleep?' An arm lends the corpse a skull, which it throws at the talkers. Finally: '(*A prodigious yawn*) Ho-hum! Me for the worms! (THE HEAD *disappears as the curtain falls*.)' In the text, Mrs Zero gets into bed and continues to talk as the curtain falls. In the 1923 production the actress provoked laughter by waiting until the end of her speech before climbing into bed beside the silent man she had verbally abused for more then ten minutes.

Among the characteristics of expressionism listed earlier, comedy is conspicuously absent – as it is from most expressionistic plays, which are usually not produced in the American commercial theatre and are usually not commercially successful if they are produced. *The Adding Machine* demonstrates that with comedy expressionism may become acceptable at the box office. But commercial appeal in no way diminishes this play's considerable artistic qualities.

'Street Scene'

Considering the critical and popular success of *Street Scene*, it may seem surprising that Rice had difficulty placing it after its completion in early 1928. Producers turned it down as undramatic, dull, confusing or sordid. One looked at the large cast list, estimated the salaries, and read no further. Finally William A. Brady, a producer of pre-First World War vintage who wanted to make a comeback, decided to gamble on the play.

Haste and chaos often characterise Broadway procedures. In November 1928 Brady set the opening date, 12 January 1929: two months to sign a director and cast and rehearse a large number of actors. Because expenses prohibited out-of-town tryouts, every production problem had to be solved during rehearsals and the show would 'open cold' on Broadway, a chilling prospect.

As director Brady signed George Cukor, who would later make such films as *The Philadelphia Story* and the Judy Garland *Star Is Born*. Casting was frenzied: hundreds of actors jammed into a packed room that provided inadequate opportunity to demonstrate their abilities. Cukor had misgivings about the play. One day he left for lunch, got another job, and did not return. With rehearsals to begin in less than two weeks, an opening night scheduled, and various directors rejecting the job, Rice offered to direct, although his only experience had been with amateurs. Justifiably, Brady hesitated to entrust a novice with a play that had a cast of fifty (some playing several roles) in a complicated setting. When Rice agreed to waive the director's fee if the play did not succeed, Brady capitulated.

Street Scene depicts a New York City street in front of a brownstone building. Exploring Manhattan for a model, Rice found what his mind's eye had seen, an ugly building at 25 West 65th Street. The designer, Jo Mielziner, agreed to its appropriateness. But a New York house does not stand isolated in a field. To eliminate adjoining houses would be unrealistic, to show them would disperse the focus. On one side of the stage Rice had a building being demolished; on the other, the windowless wall of a storage warehouse – thereby heightening the brownstone house without loss of realism. To account for the absence of traffic, a sign on the curb read 'Street Closed', a familiar sight in New York City. The side buildings also solved a design problem: like walls in an interior set and trees in a countryside, they induce the audience to overlook the sides of the proscenium arch.

Rice the director began by dropping those actors he

found unsatisfactory and who had not yet signed a contract. The large cast, combined with Brady's parsimony, forced him to choose mainly unknowns. For Rose, he engaged Erin O'Brien-Moore, who the past April had played the female lead in E. E. Cummings' *Him* at the Provincetown Playhouse. For the Jewish-Russian radical he signed Leo Bulgakov, formerly of the Moscow Art Theatre. The malicious gossip was played by Beulah Bondi, who would later act in many films, including *It's a Wonderful Life*. John Qualen, whose films would include *The Grapes of Wrath*, was the Swedish janitor.

Regardless of the complexity of production, Actors Equity Association limited rehearsals of non-musical plays to twenty-eight days. After Cukor's defection Rice had twenty-six. *Street Scene* is not set on a flat surface but has different levels and areas: floor, stoop, vestibule, visible interiors in two stories, and cellar steps. Whereas an average play might have a few dozen entrances and exits, *Street Scene* has over a hundred in the first act alone, plus crowd scenes. On a flat rehearsal floor, director Rice and his actors estimated how long it would take to climb or descend steps, where to stand in order to be visible or to avoid masking another actor, how to bring on, place and remove crowds. While none of these represents an insurmountable difficulty, together they consume much rehearsal time and require actors to attend to them as well as to characterisation and interaction. If the director is to avoid chaos at rehearsals he must plan movements and groupings in choreographic detail; the actor must be convinced the director's preparation has been accurate, that for example on the actual set he will be seen by the audience on a step and not as on the rehearsal floor be masked by actors in front of him; and actors must drill as soldiers so that their paces will take them to the right destinations. Fortunately

Rice did his homework well, the actors trusted him, and when they finally acted in Mielziner's set everything (in theatre slang) 'worked'.

The play succeeded more than anyone had dared to hope. Reviews were unanimously favourable. It ran for six hundred and one performances. Three touring companies were organised. In London its success was repeated, though censorship obliged Rice to make such insignificant cuts as 'bitch', 'Goddamn', a woman undressing at a window, and the screams of another woman in childbirth. In 1931 Samuel Goldwyn produced a film version, screenplay by Rice. Faithful to the play, the film kept the brownstone exterior prominent and avoided excursions into the rooms, but it effectively used close-ups to emphasise individuals and incidental backgrounds, and it showed the arrival of an ambulance, a traffic jam, and larger crowds than the stage could accommodate. Hollywood's Production Code Administration, a self-censorship body, obtained deletions as trivial as those in London.[5]

Frequently, naturalism avoids a single, focused, Ibsenite plot and instead presents a panorama of people in many situations. *Street Scene* contains a cross-section of New York's 1929 melting-pot: Italian, German, Swedish, Irish, Jewish-Russian; schoolteacher, student, real-estate worker, milkman, iceman, policeman, social worker, moving-man; radical, reactionary, indifferent; union member, anti-unionist. Some characters are kind, some vicious, some violent. When Rice could not develop different facets of minor characters in the text, he did so by casting against type. When the role of the bullying cab-driver went to an actor with a pleasant personality, the actor's persona added another dimension to the character.[6]

To help depict the environment, Rice introduces stray background characters unrelated to any situation. People appear and leave: a man in a dinner jacket, a dowdy woman wheeling a decrepit baby carriage, a man with a club foot, a nun. After gunfire, the crowd that forms includes non-residents of the building: a grocery boy, workmen from the warehouse next door, and people from nearby houses. The different situations form a mosaic, and Rice skilfully shifts focus from one group to another in an almost musical manner, with repetition and counterpoint of theme and character. Partly for this reason, coincidence is less prominent than it might be. Also, thematic statements are less obtrusive.

Yet the play is not merely a group of characters and situations loosely thrown together. It has two plots: a melodramatic sex triangle in which husband murders wife and lover before police catch him and a burgeoning romance between a Jewish-American boy and an Irish-American girl. Rice removes staleness from the first partly by characterisation (the wife is starved more for affection than for sex and her lover is *'prematurely bald'* and dressed in a cheap though flashy suit), partly by dramaturgy (Chekhovianly, he spreads focus to other characters not involved in this story and keeps such emotionally charged scenes as the shooting and the killer's capture offstage, stressing reaction not action). He avoids sentimentality for the second plot partly by showing it is better for the characters that each goes his separate way to self-fulfilment, partly by dramatising diverse attitudes towards mixed marriage (young Sam and Rose regard their different religions as irrelevant, but their fathers and his sister do not). Contrapuntally, Rice dramatises a happy mixed marriage between an Italian (by inference, Catholic) and a German (by inference, Lutheran). Consistent with the methods of naturalism, he does not emphasise the contrast.

The language of this naturalistic play reflects New York's

melting pot. With effective restraint, Rice employs clichés: 'I was just saying to my wife, it's not the heat I mind so much as it is the humidity' and 'If you don't like the way things is run here, why in hell don't you go back where you came from?' With equal restraint, he employs period argot: 'I haven't tried to vamp Sam' and 'I kesh ko! I kesh ko!' – the cry of an oldclothesman, 'I cash clothes', that is, pay or take cash for buying or selling them. Accents too are authentic.

Dialogue ebbs and flows from group to group, and in this naturalistic play speeches irrelevant to plot become relevant in other ways. Thus, between a scene with Rose and Sam and one with her brother, two 19-year-old girls enter, discuss a school lesson as they cross the stage, and leave. They disperse emphasis from the major figures, disguise a dramatic convenience (exit Sam, enter brother), help to sustain the flow of life, and reveal types of New Yorkers who do not live in this building. The girls do not reappear.

In naturalism environment is important, and in the drama it becomes visible as scenery. Rice's depiction of the building is precise. Since the *ugly brownstone* [. . .] *was built in the nineties*' its ornamental iron railing is *'rusted'*, the flight of wooden steps that lead to the cellar and the janitor's apartment are *'rotting'*, and so forth. He describes the city in the morning. As the milkman goes to the steps, he sees through a bedroom window a woman about to undress; she sees him and pulls down the shade; he continues on his way. A gum-chewing boy emerges from the house, throws the wrapper on the stoop, jumps down the four steps in a single leap, pulls the chewing gum from his mouth in a long ribbon, and avoids stepping on the cracks in the pavement. A woman in a nightgown appears at a window, yawns and disappears. A crying baby stops bawling.

But environment involves more than a building, movement and stage properties. Many of these characters are shaped by the same socio-economic environment as the ciphers of *The Adding Machine*. They cannot think for themselves but instead repeat empty slogans and attitudes created by non-education, maleducation, and newspapers that catering to the lowest denominator mould ideas. Verbally and physically, bigots abuse Jews; workers are proud of their strong unions but ridicule a teacher's union (to them, teaching is babysitting, not work); and they defend conventional morality, partly because they, like Zero, have a slave psychology that fears freedom and needs security. Rice's hand is not heavy. He uses humour to subvert stereotype when the Italian man advises the Irish girl to marry a rich man since it is better to have money than beauty, then adds that she should not marry the Jewish boy because Jews think only of money. Subtly, Rice explodes the cliché of moneyed Jews: his Jewish family is as poor as everyone but the widow who is evicted. This environment contains kindness as well as hatred. A woman makes chicken soup for another who has just given birth. The Italian gives money to the woman about to be evicted so that she and her children may go to the cinema. Rose comforts Sam when a bully attacks him.

Environment includes weather. *Street Scene* takes place on a hot summer day. While dialogue and stage directions refer to heat, and props include ice cream cones and fans, it is primarily actors who convey heat. They mop their faces or necks, unbutton collars, move lethargically, loosen or flap sweaty garments, and perform dozens of individually insignificant movements that collectively reveal weather.

Though the play opened in midwinter, their illusion of heat was so convincing, says Rice, that people were surprised to find cold weather when they left the theatre.

To many, naturalism means a large amount of physical detail: in theatrical terms, properties. *Street Scene* has over three hundred, including a garbage can, a glass of steaming tea, a pair of roller skates, a pipe with ashes to be knocked out, a mailman's pouch with letters, and a rack of milk bottles. These props are functional, that is to say characters use them, thereby conveying the impression of real life. While Sam and Rose discuss religion, for instance, he eats coffee cake.

Enhancing the illusion of a slice of life are the sounds of the city. I do not know whether *Street Scene* is the first drama to record and play the noises of New York but so many reviewers comment on this, they cannot have been accustomed to it. According to stage directions, such noise is constant throughout the play. Rising, falling and inter-mingling are roars of elevated trains, car horns, whistles of river boats, rattles of trucks, and sounds of fire engines, ambulances, radios, dogs and quarrelling or laughing people. '*The noises are subdued and in the background, but they never wholly cease.*' Key moments indicate exact sounds, such as an alarm clock, a piano lesson, gun shots and the tuning of a violin. During performances, in addition to 'live' sound effects, two records of city noises (trains and traffic, for instance), started a minute apart, produced an overlapping effect that dazzled audiences with lifelikeness.

Sound also comes from people. Walking on a wooden stage floor produces a different sound from walking on pavement. Rice had a thin coat of cement poured on the stage floor. Whether or not audiences recognised the sound, the actors did and were helped in creating the atmosphere of the play.

Setting, objects, movements and groupings of characters, authentic dialogue spoken authentically, the ebb and
flow of life, attitudes of people, weather, sounds of the city
– every review testifies to the veracity of this naturalistic
production of a naturalistic play. 'It is like spying upon the
neighbours with earphones and binoculars' (*New York
Evening Journal*); 'as photographic as a play can be' (*Daily
News*); 'as if the Playhouse had had its back wall removed
and the audience given a view of any commonplace street
with its teeming crowds' (*Theatre*).

Not only does naturalism focus upon environment, it also
focuses upon passions. Sex and booze provoke the murder
(the husband says he would not have acted so rashly had he
not been drinking). As he does with expressionism in *The
Adding Machine*, Rice in *Street Scene* makes naturalism
acceptable for the commercial theatre. While his environment degrades, only a few characters are entirely debased;
most are basically decent. The bullying taxi driver and his
gossiping mother are malicious bigots, but the Italian offers
an ice cream cone to the Jew whose son he advises the Irish
girl not to marry, and that son gets on well with most of the
characters. Environment has not degraded young Sam and
Rose, who strive to escape. Lust is not a remorseless drive
but a momentary respite that the wife wishes were unneces-
sary. The point is not that such a view of life is untrue (quite
the contrary), but that this type of naturalism differs from
Zola's brand, which stresses the sordid. One may emphasise a flower as well as the dirt from which it grows, and in
doing both Rice has created a naturalistic work compatible
with success in the commercial theatre.

The late director and critic Harold Clurman wisely
remarked to me that the only type of writer whose work is
consistent is a hack. Despite Rice's huge output and his

writing on assignment, he is not a hack. The quality of his work varies, as he is professional enough to recognise. While 'not ashamed' of *On Trial*, for example, this pro assesses that its distinctive use of flashbacks is a 'gimmick' and 'As for the "human interest", if it was there it was by sheet accident'. He crows at the success of *Street Scene*, including its Pulitzer Prize, because of his difficulty in persuading someone to produce it. He is also proud of plays that were not critically or financially successful: *We, the People* received cheers mainly from the balcony, where seats were inexpensive, and boos mainly from the orchestra (stalls), where seats were expensive.

He employs theatrical craftsmanship on potboilers and works of art. Understandably, his attitude towards the American commercial theatre is ambivalent. Why did he collaborate with Philip Barry on *Cock Robin*? 'We thought it would be a good idea to turn out a popular success that would enrich us both.' Yet when the Actors' Theatre, which had planned to produce *The Subway*, collapsed because of financial woes, he deplored 'the failure of another attempt to establish a permanent theatre for the production of plays of merit'. At times he complains of Broadway's subordination of art to business, emphasis on trivia, and indifference or hostility to plays with important themes and new techniques. At other times he asserts that 'There are no generally accepted objective criteria for determining whether a given play is artistic (that is, good) or inartistic (that is, bad)' and that 'A play that is prompted by the highest ideals and artistic intentions is not necessarily a better play than one written with a weather eye to the box office'.[7]

The extent to which Rice is an artist or a purveyor of commodities troubled him, probably because he is both. Sometimes he dramatically disguises the dilemma: *Dream*

Girl contains arguments about idealism and moneymaking in the field of law. Sometimes he writes about artists: *Black Sheep* (written in 1921) has a serious writer who despite critical acclaim struggles to get commercial work to survive; in *Two on an Island* a producer explains that while he knew his play would flop he did it for his salary as director, office overhead, kickbacks from makers of costumes and furniture, and possible sale of film rights. These examples demonstrate Rice's preoccupation with the subject. Sometimes he was commercially successful, sometimes not; sometimes artistically successful, sometimes not; and sometimes artistic and commercial success combined.

3
E. E. Cummings

The dramatic output of the poet E. E. Cummings is small:
three complete plays, of which two are one-acters. While
the title *Anthropos* (written 1929) indicates its subject,
Man, Cummings labels its three most talkative characters
Infrahuman Creatures; Man, who is human, is an artist.
Whereas those beneath him wear '*filthy skins*' in the cave
that is the set, Man, back towards the audience, is naked, as
the artist is when he displays his art, an emanation of
himself. He draws a sort of monster, whose model rattles,
hisses and clanks behind an upstage curtain. The Infrahumans have letters, not names: G, O and D. So that
spectators can understand, they exclaim in sequence
phrases that begin with the letters: 'Gee – that's SWELL!',
'O-BOY!', 'DE-CIDEDLY!' To manipulate the Mob, this collective god finds slogans, which are clichés: 'Time is money',
'Nothing succeeds like success', and finally 'Evolution',
which represents 'the Ford's truth', 'So help me Lenin!':
indicating that under both capitalism and communism
hollow slogans control the masses. Meanwhile, the artist

tries to create. To re-examine the 'mammoth' he draws he removes the curtain, revealing a large steamshovel – a twentiety-century mammoth, therefore the source of contemporary art. It terrifies the Infrahumans but fascinates him. Whereas Man the artist ignores the clichés of the day, he sees its reality with creative wonder, not fear.

The subtitle of *Santa Claus* (written 1945, performed 1960), 'A Morality', hints that its characters personify abstractions. As in *Anthropos* the Mob is swayable and unindividualised. The Woman is love, the Child innocence with all its insights. Death, the title character's antagonist, is that which is fearful, the destroyer. His costume is traditional: black tights with white skeleton bones and a skull-mask. Also traditional is the costume of Santa, who is likable: a giver of happiness. Because he is what Death is not, he is a living and creative force. But Death is real, Santa not. He is an invention, a fiction, thus a work of art.

Santa is crestfallen because he wants to give understanding, which no one will take. By contrast, no one wants to give what Death would take. He explains why people will not accept Santa's offer: the world of human beings is not a 'true or actual world', that is, it is not a world based on true or genuine values; people are unable to dream, blind to beauty. Thus Santa's clothes are *'motheaten'*, the red *'faded'*: what he is, symbolised by what he wears, is neglected. This world wants knowledge without understanding. Removing Santa's mask to reveal a young man's face (youth and life harmonise with Santa), Death enjoins him to forget understanding. Doffing his own mask to reveal a skull (the mask shows the truth), Death then exchanges masks with Santa. A costumed personification with an inappropriate mask, Santa does Death's work.

Through the pseudo-knowledge that lacks understanding, a Mob buys stocks in a fictitious wheelmine (a wheel

47

plus a mine equals a wheelmine) from Santa. Since two negatives make an affirmative, non-existent workers die by accident in the non-existent wheelmine. To save himself from lynching, Santa follows Death's advice to persuade the Mob he does not exist. A little girl is undeceived by his mask: 'You are Santa Claus'. If he is Santa, who does not exist, then he does not exist and is innocent of crime. The Mob disintegrates.

To impress a woman, Death persuades Santa to change costumes with him. After Death leaves, re-enter the Child who despite Santa's appearance recognises his identity. The uncorrupted Child, who has demonstrated understanding, is Santa's. The Woman, possibly the same Death wants to impress, is what Santa lacks: love. Like Santa and the Child, she has understanding: 'Knowledge has taken love out of the world', which is therefore empty, for human beings cannot be human. She gives herself to Death – or rather the appearance of Death, really Santa, who unlike Death has loved a woman. When Santa tells her he will take her 'Now and forever', she recognises the voice 'of him I loved more than my life'. As each finds love, Death dies: his corpse hangs from a pole carried by the fickle Mob, which has again turned on the wheelmine-salesman. Although the appearance of Santa dies, his antithesis really dies. Although the appearance of Death survives, what Santa represents survives. The Child embraces the Woman, who kneels before Santa, again unmasked, a young man. He is not an abstraction but a human being. With the Child revealed as theirs, the three unite in understanding and love.

'Him'

Written nineteen years before *Santa Claus*, *Him* is more

ambiguous and complex, its canvas larger. It contains twenty-one scenes, a dozen sets including a revolving room, and over a hundred roles. Uncut, as the Circle Repertory Theatre apparently staged it in New York in 1974 (with the dramatist Lanford Wilson as Him), it ran for almost four hours. Surprisingly, its four professional productions in English (the only I know about) have been in impoverished circumstances. The first, in 1928, was at O'Neill's former home, the Provincetown Playhouse, which has virtually no wing space (areas to the side of the stage) and absolutely no fly space (above the stage). Thirty actors played all the roles and Cummings himself cut the text. Twenty years later it re-emerged at the same theatre, also cut, staged by Gene Saks (later director of many Neil Simon plays and films). In 1950 Eric Bentley directed young English professionals (including Kenneth Tynan, not yet a critic, as Him) at Salzburg, Germany, where he made 'large excisions' and streamlined many speeches. 'The circumstances of production', he says, 'were primitive.' Lighting was unsoftened by coloured gelatins. Without a revolving stage, the room's walls were shifted by hand. Without enough actors for the circus freaks, painted portraits on small panels served.[1] Like the Provincetown Playhouse, the Circle Repertory Theatre is cramped. To know that this multiscenic, superspectacular, castofhundreds play (in Cummingstalk) has been produced under spartan circumstances might prompt readers to let imagination take them where it would.

Although the response to *Him* in 1928, as later, was controversial, the battle lines were not between so-called highbrow and lowbrow critics. Some reputed intellectuals loathed the play. George Jean Nathan called it 'incoherent, illiterate, preposterous balderdash', Alexander Woollcott 'pretentious and empty', resulting in 'inexpressible boredom'. Yet John Anderson of the popular New York *Journal* praised its 'eloquent delirium' whose 'babbling madness surges now and then through passages of astounding coherence and sensitive poetry' that contains 'a scalding mockery of the whole theatre'. Richard Lockridge of the popular *New York Sun* observed 'enough strikingly theatrical scenes to make half a dozen plays [. . .]. Some of them have that *meaningful* intelligibility of music.' Probably in an effort to turn controversy into good box office, the Provincetown Players published a sixteen-page pamphlet, *Him and the Critics*, collating these and similar comments, such as Stark Young's perception that the company's decision 'to allow an important poet to have his play go as he wrote it [. . .] is what justifies and distinguishes the Provincetown's existence'. During its four-week run, audiences filled the small theatre.

The appropriate distinction is not between highbrow and lowbrow drama but among avant-garde drama, popular entertainment and packaged commodity. The last is less art than merchandise and to sell the others it dulls their distinctiveness and makes them bland. *Him* fuses the avant-garde theatre of the 1920s with popular American entertainment, both in contrast to Broadway realism.[2] An admirer of such avant-garde theatre as the Erik Satie–Jean Cocteau–Pablo Picasso *Parade*, Cummings also adored such popular arts as the circus, vaudeville and ragtime music. To him, distinctions between the avant-garde and popular entertainment were 'perfectly superficial'.[3] He considered conventional commercial theatre to be as 'thoroughly dead' as the 'so-called "serious drama" '. The quintessence of art, whether abstract modernism or a burlesque show, is (he emphasises by bursting into capital letters) 'TO BE INTENSELY ALIVE'. In gaudy burlesque ' "opposites" occur *together*' and in the spectacular circus 'unbelievably skilful and inexorably beautiful and unimaginably dangerous things are continually happening'; though 'there is a little too much going on at any given moment', Cummings insists with italics that '*this is as it should be*'. In contrast to conventional theatre, the circus is intrinsically immense and never motionless. Because 'movement is the content, the subject-matter, of the circus, while bigness is its form', in it '(as in all true "works of art") content and form are aspects of a homogeneous whole'. Better than either is – and he links Aristotle with pop – that 'incredible temple of pity and terror, mirth and amazement', Coney Island, Brooklyn's huge carnival-amusement park that fuses circus and theatre. Like the theatre it fosters illusion; like the circus it provides the breathtaking. Why better than both? 'Whereas at the theatre we merely are deceived, at Coney we deceive ourselves. Whereas at the circus we are merely spectators of the impossible, at Coney we ourselves perform impossible feats.' Thus, 'the essence of Coney Island's "circus-theatre" consists in *homogeneity*. THE AUDIENCE IS THE PERFORMANCE, and vice-versa.' Not 'a box of negligible tricks' like the commercial theatre, Coney magically blends 'barkers and bally-hoomen', dizzying illusion, flashes of colours, toy cars that are screechingly real, struttingly aristocratic freaks, intricately deceptive clowns, revolving palaces and collapsing walls into a homogeneous universe.

These descriptions fit the gaudy *Him*, where opposites join, where too much is as it should be, where movement, size and diversity blend homogeneously as content and form, where with breathtaking surprises illusion lets us deceive ourselves. *Him* does not represent but *is* a Coney Island style of life. Its attractions include a carnival with a sideshow of freaks, a snake-oil salesman, a ministrel show, bursting balloons, a vaudeville act, parodies of highbrow drama, a painted panel with holes for people's heads to poke through, and a three-wall room that is and is not realistic (the set of the dialogues between Him and his mistress, Me, its walls move clockwise in each new scene so that the invisible wall of the proscenium arch surfaces and a visible wall disappears, theatricalising a convention with Coneylike surprise).

The play's language, also varied, includes reflections on art by the playwriting title character, multilingual comedy (in Paris a French headwaiter talks in French to American tourists, whom he permits to speak bad French to him, then in perfect English gives an order to an underling who responds in a short sentence that combines Italian and German), drunken gibberish ('musha pologise frien vurry drunk shdishgraysh'), and carnival spiel ('Nex we have, Madame Suzette Yvonne Hortense Jacqueline Heloise Petite duh eighteen inch Parisian doll un uncompromisin opticul inspection uv dis lady will prove tuh duh satisfaction uv all consoin dut dis lidl lady is uh poificly form pocket edition uv sheek femininity'). Its references mix diversities. Within a few speeches, Him comments on the circus and the agony of the true artist; Me's allusion to moneymaking plays provokes Him's quip, 'Keyring Comedies and Keyhole Farces'; in one speech Him connects vaudeville, film farces, commercial plays and classical tragedy: 'Time and space, a softshoe turn. The wellknown writer of scenarios, properties one million lemon pies, hero a spitball artist of the first water, much furniture everywhere, broken, pity and terror incorporated, it all comes out in the wash, happy ending, I've got the machine who's got the god?'

In 'An Imaginary Dialogue' printed on the book jacket of the first edition of *Him*, the Author declares that ' "life" is a verb of two voices – active, to do, and passive, to dream', but doing may be a type of dreaming and some have discovered 'in a mirror surrounded with mirrors [. . .] the third voice of "life", which believes itself and which cannot mean because it is'. *Him* contains all three. Him writes a play, Me dreams (part or all of *Him* may be her dream during delivery: at the start, the Doctor anaesthetises Me, whose eyes close; in the last act, they open); mirrors distort and reflect. The Doctor, recognisable, plays various roles in Act ii, at the end of which he is about to be reborn; in Act iii Me, in a dreamlike scene, gives birth. *Him* has mirrors within mirrors. While Act ii may be Me's dream, it is ostensibly a play that Him says is 'all about mirrors', written not by Him but by a character in Him's play, 'the man in the Mirror'. When Him plays a character in its last scene, the innermost mirror reflects the reflection of the outermost mirror. In this mirror surrounded with mirrors the spectator is free to choose his reflector. As at Coney Island, he becomes part of the action. *Him* does not mean anything outside its multi-mirrored self because it lives and is that meaning. Confusing? No more than Coney Island. And no less.

The genre *Him* most closely resembles is surrealism. Coining the term in his preface to the play *The Breasts of Tiresias*, Guillaume Apollinaire explains: 'When man wanted to imitate walking he created the wheel, which does not resemble a leg. [. . .] After all, the stage is no more the life it represents than the wheel is a leg.' The surrealists do not portray life realistically. Revelling in its ambiguity and irrationality, they explore life's uncharted areas, such as the unconscious, which they consider more relevant than rationalism. With the unconscious come dreams and their subjectivity, eroticism and seemingly illogical connections. As the role of the unconscious expands, so does that of the spectator, who deciphers or interprets what seems indecipherable or open to many interpretations. Most surrealist dramatists, Cummings among them, are painters and poets; they provide striking visual and verbal images. Underlying surrealism is the collage aesthetic, the juxtaposition of unrelated, heterogeneous or incongruous elements on a different, unexpected plane. The surrealists approvingly quote the nineteenth-century poet Lautréamont's example of the beautiful, 'the chance meeting of a sewing machine and an umbrella on a dissecting table'. This juxtaposition does not symbolise anything but is the thing itself. In Cummings' phrase, it 'cannot mean because it is'. The juxtaposition of incongruities displaces familiar associations. Surrealist drama surprises and disconcerts. It violates customs of time, place, linear structure. It is often comic. Surrealist dramatists call attention to theatre as theatre, spoof dramatic forms, break dramatic illusion. They delight (as the expressionists usually do not) in nonsensicality, whimsy, comedy and irony; and they love the popular arts.

'Aha!' exclaims Him, 'I see it all now: The Great American Novel (gimme a chord, professor) where for the first and only time is revealed in all its startling circularity the longlost nombril of the Middle West. (*As if quoting*) Lucy T. Wot felt That Something which is nothing like anything, and quick as everything laying her red hot pail of blackberries down in the midafternoon moonlight.' Like an orator, Him calls attention to the theatrical. With dreamlike associations the speech parodies ('Great American Novel' is a cliché), suggests a brothel (where a pianist was called 'professor') and birth ('nombril'), is obscene ('T. Wot'), makes illogical connections ('Something', 'nothing', 'anything', 'everything'), and juxtaposes incongruities ('midafternoon moonlight'). The play alternates different planes: a more or less realistic love story about Him and Me (lovers who part, then meet after he returns from Paris), three women whose dialogue mocks clichés, and satire of America. It distorts time. At the end of one scene Him asks, Are you thinking, now?' Me replies, 'Now – yes'. Two scenes later Me begins with the carryover statement, 'I am thinking'. Between, flashing by in a few moments for her, is a long carnival scene, a surrealist reverie replete with phallic images, dramatising her anxieties and fears of birth, ending with her giving birth.

Him has other scenic connections. In Act I the Him–Me scenes regularly alternate with scenes of the cliché-spouting women. It also has verbal connections. Him mentions missing a 'nonexistent trapeze' by a specific distance, $6\frac{7}{8}$ inches. While a surrealist joke, it is the same number of seconds the Soap Box Orator talks of circum-navigating the globe. And Scenes 6, 7 and 8 of Act II are the last scene in America, the Atlantic voyage, and the first scene in Europe. 'Now I lay you down not to sleep', spoken in Act III, Scene 1, echoes the last words of Act II, 'Now I lay me down to sleep'. These connections do not symbolise anything; they link seemingly disparate elements, inviting us to make what we would of them.

The three planes mentioned in the penultimate paragraph constitute interlocking levels. All contain what Cummings calls the play's 'chief motif', 'pregnancy',[4] as well as motifs of art: Me may give birth to a child, Him to a play. While the Doctor's and Me's heads protrude through a painted panel on which a physician anaesthetises a woman, three sisters rock, mouthing clichés and trivia. Their given names are what Cummings would have us do: Stop, Look and Listen, which may be Weird (their surname). Their idle chatter is the stuff of American life. Presented as meaning-less or trivial phrases, they embody rather than symbolise meaningless, trivial lives. The sisters refer to children, marriage, foetuses and gestation. They also mention the Ringling Brothers (owners of a circus that later merged with Barnum and Bailey's) and connect the concerns of Me and Him: 'Life is a matter of being born. [. . .] Art is a question of being alive.'

Act II, the play within a play that is the third level, may be Me's dream, reflecting her pregnancy and her perception of Him's play. It has nine scenes, one for each month of pregnancy, and one scene has stairs nine steps high. Fulfilling the 'gospel according to Saint Freud', announced in the last scene of Act I, it contains Freudian references: Virgo carries a dripping candle, another character speaks of a month-old baby teething on a stick of dynamite, and Me's voice says a scene made her feel as if she had swallowed a caterpillar. One scene is about fornication and castration, another about the unconscious, and the final scene ends with a man reverting to a foetal position as he prepares to be born.

Me asks what Him's play is about. Him hints that it is surrealistic ('It's about anything you like': the spectator will determine its meaning), a panorama of life in its entirety ('about nothing and something and everything'), a lampoon of theatre ('about blood and thunder and love and death'), comic (a 'rollicking farce'), and a satire of America ('the subject [. . .] is the 18th Amendment [to the Constitution, establishing Prohibition]; and right now we want to ask you, could anything be funnier?').

Each of the nine scenes is a parody. The first, in which a curtain rises and a minute later falls, mocks conventional drama. 'Was that an accident? or a scene?' Me's voice asks. 'Both', says Him. Its meaning? 'Nothing, or rather: death.' The joke 'means' nothing and death is nothingness. In Scene 2 three fat, middle-aged drunks want to play tennis, which they prefer to a virgin who tries to tempt them by repeatedly telling them they have lascivious designs on her. After they leave she laments at having to sleep alone and recites a testimonial to a laxative. Such is *sexus Americanus*. Scene 3 has a Soap Box Orator try to sell a scientific product, 'radium', to a mob to cure a disease called 'cinderella' (the myth is an American syndrome) as well as such ailments as toothache, mumps, stuttering, rheumatism, pyorrhea and hernia. Exploring the fashionable subject of identity, Scene 4 has characters exchange masks, spoofing O'Neill's *The Great God Brown* (one character's real face resembles another's masked face, which looks like the Doctor, who also appears). Characters in Scene 5, a minstrel show, sing 'Frankie and Johnie'. Drumbeats substitute for obscenities: 'Frankie she went to the parlourhouse/she looked in the window so high/and there she saw her Johnie/just a –.– Fanny Frye/he was a man/and he done her wrong.' Though she will bury him, she vows to bring back the 'Best part of the man/who done me wrong' – which she does, scandalising a moral vigilante in the audience who tries to stop the show. Scene 6 lampoons Freudian psychology, then the rage in New York, and Americans' fear of the unconscious, which is carried in a closed trunk. Scene 7 ridicules Babbits, whose language, reflecting their lives, is devalued, meaningless, for example: 'What's new? – Nothing. Married? – Uh-huh.' Scene 8 uses burlesque – the set is an ancient, luxurious Roman villa as conceived by the Old Howard (a Boston burlesque house) – to satirise Italian fascists, whom it reduces to flamboyant homosexuals. The scene has no Americans but at its end Him's voice mocks Him's native country, whose Spirit of 1776 it calls 'a man with a flag a man with a fife and a drummerboy – caption: General Debility Youthful Errors and Loss of Manhood'. Despite the suffering of the masses in Scene 9, this scene too is comic: a parody of such expressionistic plays as Ernst Toller's *Man and the Masses*, whose mobs sway rhythmically. One tip-off to the humour is patterlike dialogue ('I have nothing to eat.' 'Why don't you eat nothing then?'), another the preposterous notion that though ten thousand people demonstrated in front of the American's hotel, he noticed nothing unusual.

An artist devoted to his art, Him ignores Me, who, understanding life intuitively, feels rather than thinks. Cummings sketches their conflict: 'Him's deepest wish is to compose a miraculously intense play-of-art – Me's underlying ambition is to be entirely loved by someone through whom she may have a child. He loves, not herself, but the loveliness of his mistress; she loves, not himself, but the possibility of making a husband out of a lover.'[5] They are therefore at cross-purposes. Although Him turns 'pistol' to 'Pistil. The female organ of a flower' and mentions 'Stamen is what you thought, it contains the pollen', no speech is explicit enough to clarify whether Him is aware of Me's pregnancy. Nor is it clear that Me is pregnant or has a child. While the carnival scene that flashes through Me's mind alludes to pregnancy (nine exhibits, a nine-foot Giant, an enormously fat woman, a King of *Born*eo) and ends with Me giving birth, these are thoughts, possibly but not necessarily distorted memories. The birth is ambiguous: Me holds the child proudly but Him cries in terror and the crowd in rage. And for all we know, she has an abortion or the child is stillborn.

Two matters are clear. First, Him is so absorbed in his art he is oblivious to reality, which is not on the stage of this unrealistic play but in the audience. At the end of Act III, Scene 1 Him leaves Me's room through the invisible door in the fourth Wall. He stands on the spectators' side, facing them, but no stage direction indicates he sees them. In the last scene, when Cummings changes the rules of fourth-wall realism by having Me point to the invisible wall and the real people beyond it, she – intuitively in touch with reality – sees them; Him does not. She says that they are 'pretending that this room and you and I are real'. 'I wish I could believe this', says Him. All he can do is stare, not at the audience as Me does, but '*at the invisible wall*'. Him's world is the stage, the world of art. Second, Him is a true artist. In a thematically important statement that echoes Cummings' own comments, Him declares:

> Damn everything but the circus! [. . .] And here I am, patiently squeezing fourdimensional ideas into a twodimensional stage, when all of me that's anyone or anything is in the top of a circus tent. [. . .] The average 'painter' 'sculptor' 'poet' 'composer' 'playwright' is a person who cannot leap through a hoop from the back of a galloping horse, make people laugh with a clown's mouth, orchestrate twenty lions. [. . .] But imagine a human being who balances three chairs, one on top of another, on a wire, eighty feet in air with no net underneath, and then climbs into the top chair, sits down, and begins to swing. [. . .] I am that. [. . .] I feel only one thing, I have only one conviction; it sits on three chairs in Heaven.

This 'it' which is Him rests upon three facts: 'I am an Artist, I am a Man, I am a Failure – it rocks and it swings and it smiles and it does not collapse tumble or die because it pays no attention to anything except itself. [. . .] I watch this trick, I am this trick [. . .]. I whisper: An artist, a man, a failure, MUST PROCEED.' The true artist, not the pseudo-artist, agonises over his art. The true artist compares himself and his high art to a circus acrobat who performs daring and impossible feats aloft; he is above the mob, to whom he pays no attention, for he is self-absorbed; he recognises that he examines his art and is his art; he feels compelled to proceed, notwithstanding possible disaster (he lacks a safety net).

In a programme note for the first production, Cummings issues a 'WARNING': *Him* 'isn't comedy or tragedy or a farce or a melodrama or a revue or a moving picture or any other convenient excuse for "going to the theatre" '. Thus, do not approach it in terms of any theatrical stereotype. Because *Him* is a play, 'let it PLAY with you'. Do not 'worry because it's not like something else – relax, stop wondering what it's all "about" – like many strange and familiar things, Life included, this PLAY isn't "about", it simply is. [. . .] Don't try to enjoy it, let it try to enjoy you. DON'T TRY TO UNDERSTAND IT, LET IT TRY TO UNDERSTAND YOU.' In other words, don't approach *Him* with the intellectual equipment you usually bring to intellectual drama. Let *Him* wash over you as you would let a circus do and relax as you would at a carnival-amusement park like Coney Island. If you try to enjoy it, you probably will not; if you try to understand it, you probably will not. Cummings says not that it is incomprehensible but that you can comprehend it by not trying to do so in conventional ways.

Aiming for direct communication, Cummings' theatrical arsenal includes techniques of such non-intellectual theatre as minstrel shows and carnivals. Like Coney Island, like surrealist drama, *Him* is not about something but is itself. Conventional theatre has accustomed us to regard burlesque and speeches on art, lowbrow culture and highbrow dialogue, as separable from each other. Whereas conventional theatre is tidy, the divertingly diverse *Him* is not. At times audiences become confused when a play refuses to attach itself to one style or convention and remain within its limitations. When styles and conventions shift dazzlingly, blend instantaneously, part again – when they 'turn on a sixpence' in the words of British dramatist Peter Barnes, whose plays resemble *Him* in this respect – the result can be absorbing, enjoyable, and comprehensible to those who do not try to enjoy it but let it try to enjoy them, who do not try to understand it but let it try to understand them.

As Michael Feingold, who reviewed the Circle Repertory Theatre's 1974 revival (*Village Voice*), perceives: '*Him* is one of those plays that nobody reads much – it isn't an easy read and somehow never quite makes it onto the American Literature syllabi – and, therefore, nobody performs it much. Every time someone does, however, it plays so well and sounds as freshly on the ears that you wonder why it isn't a repertory staple.' Although its scope is large, it has been mounted inexpensively. Perhaps one day it will make it on to the American Literature syllabi and become a repertory staple.

4
George S. Kaufman and Moss Hart

Between 1918 and 1945, chiefly in tandem with other writers, including Edna Ferber and Marc Connelly, George S. Kaufman had thirty-five plays and musicals produced on Broadway. Probably his most successful collaborator, the one with whom the public usually associates him, Moss Hart worked on eight. At least once, Kaufman called him his favourite collaborator.[1]

Although Kaufman did not direct every play he wrote, he directed the first productions of all he wrote with Hart. Evidently a superb director of comedy, he had a masterful sense of timing. In *George Washington Slept Here* (1940), about New Yorkers who move into a ramshackle country house, a girl wearing a bathing suit and a picturesque hat entered a room in which several men were talking to each other. Immediately the conversation stopped, she slowly climbed eight steps, turned a corner and left, whereupon conversation immediately resumed. As it did, the audience invariably burst into laughter. During a show's run, Kaufman would unexpectedly turn up to see whether it had deteriorated. On one occasion he posted a cast announcement that is now legendary: '11 A.M. rehearsal tomorrow to remove all improvements to the play since the last rehearsal'.[2]

Frequently Kaufman is – and Kaufman and Hart are – considered witty authors who satirically demolish their targets. Yet their comic dialogue is less wit, which is elegant and polished, than it is wisecrack: a bluntly derisive comment that is distinctively American. As Kaufman admits, he does not compose satire, which he supposedly defined as 'what closes on Saturday night'. Instead, he and Hart write spoofs. They poke good-natured fun at human foibles and institutions, not aggressively denounce them, as satirists do. At bottom they are one with their audiences and do not seriously threaten their targets. Perhaps a key to their commercial success is that their dialogue and viewpoint give the appearance of acid but are basically sentimental.

In *Once in a Lifetime* (1930) three small-time vaudeville comics, seeing a unique opportunity to break into the big time, palm themselves off as elocution teachers in Hollywood, which the recent arrival of sound (1927) has thrown into disarray; among other problems, producers have discovered that virile-looking male stars have effeminate speech, beautiful women squeaky voices, and both poor diction. Since talkies were luring audiences from stage plays, reviews were almost obscene in approving Kaufman and Hart's, or K & H's, lampoon: 'snarling satire' (*Billboard*) that 'conceals rocks in the [custard] pies' it hurls at Hollywood (*New York Sun*). Evidence that satire is too strong a term for their good-humoured fun, Hollywood filmed the play two years later. The rockless pies proved profitable.

I'd Rather Be Right (1937), with songs by Richard

Rodgers and Lorenz Hart, wraps its comic fists in padded gloves. It pokes mild fun at then-President Franklin D. Roosevelt, played by that Yankee Doodle Dandy, George M. Cohan, and it affectionately mocks such safe subjects as budget-balancing. Essentially, it aims to delight, not upset, Broadway audiences. Thus, the FDR of K & H can say during the Depression, 'There *are* things to worry about, but [. . .] there's something in this country – a sort of spirit that holds us all together – that always sees us through.' What matters is not an individual president but rather '(*with a wave of his hand, he indicates the multitude*) You!'

Sentimentality underlies *The Fabulous Invalid* (1938), the theatre, which often considered to be dying has always recovered. A leading man and woman die after opening night, then learn that as God realises an actor's death is special, one who dies in the theatre may elect not to go to heaven but 'hang around' the theatres and see plays for eternity or until the theatre dies. K & H treat the new ghosts and us to a series of impersonations, including David Warfield in Belasco's *The Music Master* and George M. Cohan singing 'Give My Regards to Broadway' from his *Little Johnny Jones*. Eugene O'Neill receives an obligatory moment (from *Anna Christie*) but the great bulk of the selections recalls the complaint of Shaw's Don Juan (*Man and Superman*), that hell is like perpetually attending the first acts of fashionable plays. Most of the works K & H represent are long-forgotten, unlamented, fashionable trifles. At the end, an idealistic young director in a pep talk to his cast insists that the theatre will not die. 'It's important to keep alive a thing that can lift men's spirits above the everyday reality of their lives. We mustn't let that die.' With unintentional irony, a description of his uplifting play concludes K & H's: a combination living room-dining room in a small midwestern town, the set has a cheap piano, a sideboard, a sofa, and a table set for supper. Although the ghosts are '*enchanted*' at this renewal of dramatic art, we who are quick might sigh at what promises to be the bland realism of conventional American drama.

K & H's other works are also sentimental. Sheridan Whiteside, the titular *Man Who Came to Dinner* (1939) – who tripped, presumably broke his legs, stays long after dinner, and insults almost everyone in sight – helps the young son and daughter of his host do what they want, not what their reactionary father wants, and after trying to stop his secretary's marriage, for he wants her to remain in his employ, he relents and enables her to get her man. Pompous and overbearing to the *n*th degree, Whiteside is at heart an okay guy. The atypically earnest drama *The American Way* (1939), which dramatises that if you work hard you can succeed in this free country, is cautious: its theme is anti-Hitler and its German-American protagonist is killed by Bundists, but neither Hitler nor Bund is mentioned. Anticipating Harold Pinter's *Betrayal* by over forty years (its scenes go backward in time), *Merrily We Roll Along* (1934) seems to be unsentimental, since it depicts a young dramatist's loss of youthful ideals as he adapts to the requirements of the Broadway marketplace, but its target is safe (would anyone favour loss of ideals?) and it permits one to regard wistfully one's own adaptation to life.

This catalogue of sentimentality in K & H's plays aims less to condemn them than to define their limitations. In terms of theatricality and comic entertainment they have much merit. Big curtains often close their scenes. Act I of *George Washington* ends with a storm, Act III with the approach of a hurricane. *The American Way* is spectacular: a cast of over two hundred and fifty, including extras, with such scenes as the arrival of European immigrants at dawn at Ellis Island, with the Statute of Liberty in the morning mist; and a theatricalisation of America's entry into the First World War that anticipates Joan Littlewood's *Oh, What a Lovely War!* A boy sings and plays 'Row, Row, Row' on a mandolin and is joined by others whose voices blend into the sound of a brass band playing 'Tipperary' as banners proclaim such slogans as 'UNCLE SAM WANTS YOU FOR THE ARMY' and 'OUT TO LICK THE KAISER'. Hollywood opulence brightens *Lifetime*, one of whose sets is decorated in *'Early de Mille'*, which means *'Gold-encrusted walls, heavy diamond-cut chandelier, gold brocade hangings and simply impossible settees and chairs'*. The opening scene of *Merrily* is an expensively furnished Long Island home, *'the kind of room you have often seen as a full-page illustration in* Town and Country', with guests in full evening dress. Although *Dinner* is set in a middle-class Ohio home, prodigious name-dropping conveys worldwide glamour, including telephone calls from H. G. Wells and Walt Disney, Christmas gifts from Shirley Temple and W. Somerset Maugham, and a letter dictated to Mahatma Gandhi, whom Whiteside addresses, 'Dear Boo-Boo'.

As the last example suggests, K & H's chief asset is comedy. Foremost are debunking wisecracks. When a character in *Merrily* tells Julia, 'I think you write just about the best stories I ever read. That one about the boy and the girl – I read it over and over', she asks, 'Didn't you get it the first time?' To the enthusiastic exclamation 'Just think, Annabelle! George Washington slept here. George Washington!' she looks about, then retorts, 'Martha wasn't a very good housekeeper'. Some jokes employ double meaning, a form of irony. In *Lifetime*, film-makers boast of their ability to make instantaneous decisions: 'That's the way we do things out here – no time wasted on thinking!'

When the mother of Susan, an awful actress, observes, 'it isn't so easy out here, even if you're the kind of actress Susan is,' her acting coach drily remarks, 'It's even harder if you're the kind of actress Susan is'. Master of invective is Sheridan Whiteside, whose first words, after he looks at his host's family, are: 'I may vomit'. He tells his nurse to 'read the life of Florence Nightingale and learn how unfitted you are for your chosen profession' and addresses her as 'Miss Bed Pan' (as he especially demonstrates, K & H's comedy also derives from character). Like him, his secretary employs put-down, a form of flyting. After her rival in love picks up a book from a table and asks, 'Have you read this, Maggie? Everybody was reading it on the boat. I hear you simply can't put it down', she replies, '*I* put it down – right there'.

In *Lifetime* K & H comically reduce real catastrophe to filmdom. Recalling her grandfather, a character says, 'He was in the Civil War'. Recalling *The Birth of a Nation*, another asks, 'The Civil War – didn't D. W. Griffith make that?' Reductiveness abounds in *I'd Rather Be Right*, where the President's authority is debased (his mother asks him to 'fix' a traffic violation ticket of a friend's daughter) and budget-balancing gives small expenditures the same value as large (the entry 'Ice cream, twenty-five cents' directly follows 'Two battleships, a hundred and fifty million dollars').

Often the plays employ absurd incongruities and mis-understandings. The Secretary of State tells the President that if they hurry the cabinet meeting they could all see the new Marx Brothers film. After an actor costumed as a Bishop demands a copy of the *Racing Form*, an actress dressed as a Bridesmaid asks, 'Where the hell's the bishop?' and on finding him requests a case of gin. An extra responds to news of a casting call for prostitutes: 'Say, I'm going out there! Remember that prostitute I did for Paramount?' 'Yah, but that was silent. This is for talking prostitutes.' In *George Washington* the maid asks for the night off to see a young man. Since house guests are about to arrive in a few hours the mistress refuses, suggesting she see him next week. 'No, I *can't*,' 'Of course you can.' '*Why* can't you see him next week?' 'He's getting married.' K & H do not neglect visual comedy. The new homeowner is gleeful: 'Boy, can you imagine that fireplace with a great big roaring fire! (*He sticks his head into the fireplace, trying to peer up the flue*) Ow! (*He emerges with both eyes closed and his face covered with soot*)'.

K & H are masterful parodists. One character in *Dinner* spoofs Harpo Marx, who is silent on screen. They call him by another musical instrument, Banjo (his brothers are Wacko and Sloppo). K & H succeed in this undertaking (difficult since the original is so funny) by having him look and behave like Harpo but speak like Groucho (Kaufman collaborated on several Marx Brothers films, including *A Night at the Opera* and *Horsefeathers*). Thus, enter Banjo, '*a pixie-like gentleman*', carrying Whiteside's nurse, whom he repeatedly kisses: 'I love you madly – madly! Did you hear what I said – madly! Kiss me! Again! don't be afraid of my passion. Kiss me! I can feel the hot blood pouring through your varicose veins. [. . .] Come to my room in half an hour and bring some rye bread.' In *Lifetime* K & H distort preposterously what in real life is sufficiently exaggerated. Hollywood's idea of originality may take the form of remaking a successful film of many years past; here, the dumb vaudevillian George does so by accidentally picking up the wrong script; critics consider the film a triumph because it reverts to values unfortunately forgotten. Sometimes critics praise ineptitude because it seems

deliberately to contrast with the gloss one habitually sees:
George casts Susan, as dopey as he is, in the lead; reviews
praise her clumsiness as realism. He forgets to turn on the
lights when he shoots scenes; critics applaud artistic
suggestiveness that permits audiences to imagine more
than one could show.

As in conventional comedy, the possibility of real pain or
suffering does not arise, even in *Dinner*. Before Act I ends,
the doctor reveals that Whiteside's legs are unbroken: he
examined the wrong X-rays. Also conventionally, the
likeable people succeed: though stupid George is
goodhearted, so despite his bumbling he wins Susan and is
promoted by the studio.

'You Can't Take It With You'

In terms of critical acclaim (including the Pulitzer Prize),
public response (initial run in 1936 and frequency of
revivals), and screen adaptation (including an Academy
Award as Best Film of 1938), *You Can't Take It With you* is
K & H's most successful collaboration. It focuses on the
Vanderhof-Sycamore family: in today's argot, lovable
kooks. Comic eccentricities merge with unabashed sentimentality. Ignoring the world around them, America in the
Depression, its members do what they want – to no one's
injury. A typical review of the first production contrasts the
real world, 'in which the sanity usually associated with
sunshine is sadly overvalued', with the 'moonstruck' world
of these 'gloriously mad', 'contented', and 'daffy mortals,
as lovable as they are laughable' (*New York Post*).

Thirty-five years earlier, Grandpa Vanderhof decided
that success in business took too much time and gave him

no pleasure. He summarily quit and has since spent his time having fun: playing darts, visiting the zoo and commence- ments at Columbia University, and collecting stamps and pet snakes. In his household, a stage direction informs, '*you do as you like, and no questions asked*'. What everyone likes, a variant of a Jonsonian humour, is harmless. The snakes are in a safe solarium. The matronly Penny Syca- more, who occasionally paints, mainly writes plays: because someone once mistakenly delivered a typewriter. Her husband Paul, in collaboration with Mr De Pinna, an iceman who decided to stay, manufactures fireworks in the basement. One daughter, Essie, makes candy to sell to neighbours and eat at home; she also studies ballet under the tutelage of Kolenkhov, a boisterous Russian émigré who admits she is awful but who arrives regularly for lessons and dinner. Essie's husband Ed plays the xylophone and happily works a printing press for menus and messages in the candy boxes; since his pleasure derives from printing attractive type, not the actual words, he gets equal satisfac- tion from running off 'meat' and slogans he happens to find, such as 'Dynamite the White House!' Here, disorder is the norm: 'What time is it? 'I don't know. Anyone know what time it is?' 'Mr. De Pinna might know.' 'It was about five o'clock a couple of hours ago.' With Grandpa's statement of Grace before dinner – 'Well, Sir, we've been getting along pretty good for quite a while now and we're certainly much obliged. Remember, all we ask is just to go along and be happy in our own sort of way. Of course we want to keep our health, but as far as anything else is concerned, we'll leave it to You. Thank You' – any question that these loonies are basically Good Folks vanishes.

The title reflects Grandpa's view: since you cannot take money with you when you die, you might as well enjoy life, not work as a drudge. Depression and recession audiences seem to find this escapist view very amiable (as I write, in 1983, the play is again a Broadway hit). Furthermore, according to Grandpa, if everyone relaxed as he and his family do 'there wouldn't *be* times like these. [. . .] Life is simple and kind of beautiful if you let it come to you. But the trouble is, people forget that.' In the business world is 'fighting, and scratching, and clawing. Regular jungle.' Leave it behind and relax, says he. Since previous exposition explains that he receives income from investment property which lets him relax and employ a black servant, what registers here is his stance against moneymaking in favour of pleasure – a safe stance, a safe object of derision.

The fun that derives from the madcap requires contrast with seriousness and real life. Another daughter, Alice, conventionally works as secretary to a Wall Street firm owned by Kirby. In a climactic second-act scene the stuffy, joyless Wall Street family visits the Vanderhof-Sycamore home. The reason, standard in plays and films of the 1930s, is romance between the secretary and the boss's son, Tony. When Alice invites the Kirby family for dinner, Tony purposely brings them on the wrong night so that they can see her family as it really is, not as it might behave when it wants to produce a good impression. As Alice predicts, the result is disastrous. Yet love wins and the opposition of Tony's father proves short-lived: once a budding saxaphonist, he still keeps an instrument in his closet, and he is impressed by Grandpa's battle with the Internal Revenue Service, which tries to collect taxes he refuses to pay. The IRS stops because he gave his name to someone who died and is therefore officially dead. As usual in comedy, the young couple override all obstacles to mating and Good Folks avoid imprisonment. From before the Depression to beyond the hippy era, Americans have admired individualists who, thumbing their noses at political and economic powers, believe that if good-natured people act as they wish then all will turn out well. In this amiable comedy the individualists simply ignore society in favour of an alternative way of life or, in today's term, lifestyle.

Through this family K & H poke fun at conventional whipping-boys, Wall Street and government. In a free-association game that Mrs Sycamore persuades the Kirby parents to play, Mrs Kirby says 'dull' to the word 'honeymoon' and 'Wall Street' to 'sex'. An IRS agent, Henderson, tries to persuade Grandpa to pay his income taxes. Because he receives something if he pays money in a store, Grandpa wants to know what he receives from the government. According to Henderson, he gets protection from foreign powers which might invade America and take everything he has. 'Oh', says Grandpa, 'I don't think they're going to do that.' When the IRS man mentions the cost of naval battleships, Grandpa points out that their last use was in the Spanish-American War, from which Americans only got Cuba, 'and we gave that back'. Henderson demands, 'what about Congress, and the Supreme Court, and the President? We've got to pay *them*, don't we?' Says Grandpa, '(*ever so calmly*) Not with my money – no sir.' When I saw the film revival in late 1982 the audience responded with laughter and applause.

A family like this provides numerous opportunities for comic incongruity. One reason Grandpa enjoyed the commencement at Columbia University is: 'much funnier speeches than they had last year'. A sustained comically incongruous scene occurs when Kolenkhov introduces an émigré Grand Duchess who wears an old dinner gown and a tacky evening wrap trimmed with motheaten fur. Mrs Sycamore curtsies to the floor and catches a chair before she falls down. Essie does a curtsey that '*merges the Dying Swan with an extremely elaborate genuflection*'. De Pinna bows to the floor, where he stays until told to rise. Invited to be seated, the Duchess asks, 'What time is dinner?' and explains, 'I do not mean to be rude, but I must be back at the restaurant by eight o'clock. I am substituting for another waitress.' She discourses on the King of Sweden and Rasputin, then grandly enters the kitchen to help prepare the meal, since she enjoys cooking. What she will cook, however, is hardly aristocratic: blintzes.

The play contains many sight gags. For instance, Mrs Sycamore uses a kitten as a paperweight. Each time she completes a page she removes it from the typewriter, mechanically picks up the kitten, puts the page on the pile beneath, and replaces the kitten. When the Kirby family enters in full evening regalia it sees Mrs Sycamore in an artist's smock painting bald, middle-aged De Pinna, who wears a Roman toga and carries a discus; Essie in ballet costume, dancing while Ed plays the xylophone and Kolenkhov loudly directs her; an actress lying drunk on the floor; and Grandpa playing darts.

K & H do not neglect slapstick. To demonstrate his conviction that the elder Kirby might be a great wrestler, Kolenkhov grabs his arms, quickly kicks his legs from under him, throws him to the floor, and plunges upon him. The Act II finale is particularly farcical. Because of Ed's printed slogans, government agents arrive to arrest him as a dangerous anarchist, but they prevent De Pinna from going to the basement to retrieve his pipe, which accidentally sets off the fireworks:

> *It is a whole year's supply of fireworks – bombs, big crackers, little crackers, skyrockets, pin wheels, everything. The house is fairly rocked by the explosion.*
>
> *In the room, of course, pandemonium reigns.* MRS. KIRBY *screams; the* G-MAN *drops* [the actress] *right where*

he stands and dashes for the cellar, closely followed by MR.
DE PINNA *and* PAUL; PENNY *dashes for her manuscripts and*
ED *rushes to save his xylophone.* KOLENKHOV *waves
his arms wildly and dashes in all directions at once;
everyone is running this way and that.*

All except one. The exception, of course, is GRANDPA,
who takes all things as they come. GRANDPA *just says 'Well,
well, well!' – and sits down.*

Reviews praised Kaufman's direction of the original
production not only for his orchestrated traffic management but also for his contrast of breakneck speed and
relaxation (as contrast, the latter enables a director to
achieve the effect of the former). However, Kaufman's
significant directorial accomplishment was an appearance
of 'bright innocence' from the entire family (*New
Republic*). Apart from indicating they were accustomed to
what others consider outrageous, the actors' casualness
amused because they 'never let anyone know that they
consider themselves either odd or funny'. They behaved
insanely 'in the most straightfaced, natural manner', without smiling or overplaying. Particularly impressive was the
Grandpa of Henry Travers (whose many film roles include
James Stewart's guardian angel in *It's a Wonderful Life*):
'lovably gentle' with 'sweetness', 'a serenity and a goodness' (*New York Post*). Josephine Hull gave Penny 'the
fluttering amusement of a happy half-wit' (*New York
Evening Journal*). Paula Trueman played Essie 'suavely'
but 'unconsciously forlorn' (*Brooklyn Daily Eagle*).

In Frank Capra's 1938 film, which expanded the lov-
ableness of the Vanderhof-Sycamore clan (by showing
their neighbours' fondness for them) and the humanity of
the Kirby family (thus making more believable the father's
capitulation), the eccentrics likewise did not act as if they

knew they were zany but behaved as if they were normal. More clearly than the play, the film reassured Depression audiences that though they were poor in material wealth they were rich in humanity, therefore superior to the wealthy, who at the end embrace the Good Folks' home-spun warmth. As the older Kirby, the wide-girthed Edward Arnold found moments to unstarch his shirt, such as secretly appreciating his son's irreverence towards business – providing character not caricature. James Stewart acted Tony in his best 'Aw, shucks' manner that combined naïve befuddlement with the smugness of the cat who swallowed the canary. As Alice, Jean Arthur's blend of an innocent appearance and a sexy voice made Tony's infatuation thoroughly believable. As Grandpa, Lionel Barrymore had a folksy, down-home manner; as Penny, Spring Byington was innocently oblivious to her daffiness. The self-confidence with which Ann Miller, a good dancer, moved helped persuade one that Essie lacked talent.

By common consent, the 1965 New York revival, its most notable, was 'an ensemble success' (*Village Voice*). Ellis Rabb recreated 'the stage style of the past', with performances that were 'not mimicry or burlesque but *duplication* of the old style'. As Alice, Rosemary Harris 'actually *became* an actress starring in a 1936 comedy' (*Women's Wear Daily*). As performed by Harris and Clayton Corzatte (Tony), the romantic scenes 'take on an unexpected delicacy', for they succeed in 'wringing the gush out of [the sentimentality] and making it believable'. They enact their shy avowal of love with 'the grace of an airy wry ballet' (*New York Times*). Robert Brustein (*New Republic*) describes it: when Harris and Corzatte 'plight their troth while dancing to a warbly vocal of "These Foolish Things", part into an elaborate fox-trot break, and then return into an embrace, with Miss Harris lifting one leg daintily behind her – it is a moment of cultural history as evocative as an old Grant–Hepburn movie.' As Grandpa, the 'Serene, patient and content' Donald Moffat 'says grace more as conversation than ritual prayer' (*New York World-Telegram and Sun*).

The ambience of *You Can't Take It With You* resembles an urban Forest of Arden or a parlour version of the below-stairs world in *Twelfth Night*. As mentioned, the Vanderhof-Sycamore home is a place of revelry and merriment, where the work ethic and ordinary constraints upon human behaviour do not exist. In the Shakespearean plays, reality enters. Winters in Arden are cold and when the exiles of *As You Like It* receive a chance to leave it for court all but Jaques do so. In *Twelfth Night* Sirs Toby and Andrew get a thrashing and the latter loses the fair lady. Despite happy ends, real life is unconquered. Not so, *You Can't Take It With You*, where the real world capitulates to the topsyturvydom of the loonies' world. The IRS may even give Grandpa a refund for unpaid taxes. The Wall Street tycoon who true to comedy's convention blesses the young couple is drawn into the world of the eccentrics, for he admires Grandpa's victory over the IRS. *You Can't Take It With You* is not Shakespearean saturnalia; it is American escapism.

5
Maxwell Anderson

Eugene O'Neill began the creation of a theatrical environment that made possible the career of Maxwell Anderson. Without the earthy dialogue of O'Neill's *Anna Christy* Broadway may not have been receptive to the salty phrases of Anderson's and Laurence Stallings' *What Price Glory* (1924), much of which is comic. Without O'Neill's efforts to create tragedy, Anderson's vision of poetic tragedy, a contrast to O'Neill's prose, might not have been realised on stage. Comedy and tragedy suggest Anderson's range, which embraces melodrama, fantasy and social protest. Woven throughout his variegated drama are views of individualism; social institutions that thwart, oppress and plunder individuals; rebels who defy society; and questions of integrity.

To Anderson, theatre aims to 'hold up to our regard what is admirable in the human race'. It 'is a religious institution devoted entirely to the exaltation of the spirit of man'.[1] Unless good defeats evil, the 'moral atmosphere' is unhealthy (p. 26). In tragedy the hero, learning through suffering, becomes a better person (p. 61). Tragedy's perennial theme is 'victory in defeat', its message' that 'men are better than they think they are' (p. 90). While these views are lofty, they frequently result in sentimentality and pious attitudinising. While few would agree that evil must triumph, a tragic view of life or an undistorted depiction of reality should permit either that possibly or else greater ambiguity than Anderson proposes. Does Euripides' Medea, for instance, become a better person? Is the message of *Medea*, of of Euripides' darker, more ambiguous tragedy *The Bacchae*, that people are better than they imagine themselves to be? With Anderson, by contrast, we too often enter the world of Uplift.

Although his heroes are individualists, frequently opposed to a corrupt society, his plays are not revolutionary calls to action. According to Anderson, one must protest injustice despite the futility of such protest. Realistic as his plays are in psychology and social ambience, they are usually romantic or defeatist; heroic gestures have no social consequences; and noble causes are abandoned, lost, or if won corrupted by those in power.

In its preface, Anderson and Stallings call *What Price Glory* 'a play of war as it is, not as it has been presented theatrically for thousands of years'. Therefore, the soldiers' speech is 'consistently interlarded with profanity. [. . .] *What Price Glory* may seem bold.' In its time it did. The realistic obscenity – frequent use of 'hell', 'God damn', and 'son-of-a-bitch' – was probably one of Stallings' contributions: unlike Anderson he served in the First World War and Anderson's solo plays about the Second World War have less profanity than *What Price Glory*. *The Eve of St. Mark* (1912) only occasionally uses the obscenities quoted and it employs such polite terms as 'sexual intercourse'. *Storm Operation* (1944) bowdlerises with inaccurate definitions of Army acronyms, including 'Snafu. S.N.A.F.U. Situation Normal – all mucked up'. Avoiding language unacceptable on Broadway in the 1940s, Anderson rhymingly suggests that he really knows the word.

A commercial success, *What Price Glory* demonstrates the truth of American Civil War General Sherman's statement 'War is hell' (one soldier holds 'half his guts in his bare hands' while 'hollering for somebody to turn him loose so he could shoot himself'), but while satiric (to a general's enthusiastic 'We want to go in there and run 'em out. We want to give 'em steel', a battlefield captain responds ironically, 'We? Staff going in there too, General?') the play is not anti-war. It subordinates war to romantic shenanigans: the rivalry of colourful, manly Captain Flagg and Sergeant Quirt for the favours of a tart, Charmain. Only Act II is at the front, where their major concern is to return to her, which they do in Act III: with farcical exits, entrances and near-encounters. Ordered to the trenches again, the rivals leave. The curtain line is Quirt's: 'What a lot of God damn fools it takes to make a war! Hey, Flagg, wait for baby!' Despite the assertion of war's folly, male bonding gives a cheerfully upbeat end that inserts fun into folly, thereby minimalising the horrors dramatised in Act II.

The hoboes who are the chief characters of *Outside Looking In* (1925), a title that indicates their social status, frequently comment on society's injustices: most vividly, the racial wrongs towards a black hobo. Although most of them are accustomed to fighting and killing, one of the toughest turns sentimental at the end: he persuades the others not to flee the police but to remain in order to stall them, thus permitting the escape of a young man and woman who had murdered her stepfather (who seduced her, which led to prostitution, then jail).

Rebels against and victims of social injustice are key

figures in *Gods of the Lightning*, written with Harold Hickerson, based on a famous and still controversial case. In April 1920 thieves killed a paymaster and guard in Massachusetts. Two Italian anarchists who may have been draft evaders, Nicola Sacco and Bartolomeo Vanzetti, were arrested. Patriotic and anti-radical feeling ran high. While evidence against them was circumstantial, while they protested their innocence, and while a condemned criminal, Celestino Madeiros, confessed that he participated in the crime (but did not murder anyone) and that the pair was innocent, they were convicted. After the governor refused clemency they were executed in August 1927. This is basically the plot of *Gods of the Lightning*, which opened fourteen months later. The defendants are James Macready, an organiser for the IWW (Industrial Workers of the World, sometimes called wobblies) and Dante Capraro, an atheist and anarchist. The District Attorney intimidates and blackmails witnesses to testify falsely. A prejudiced judge permits misleading evidence to go to the jury.

The play contains much social commentary. How do the police obtain evidence against radicals? 'A cop jumps on the running board and tosses a gun into the car and then they start to arrest the bunch for carrying concealed weapons.' Courts and police function 'to protect capital and keep the working man in his place!' Whenever laws, including the Bill of Rights, 'might be to the working man's advantage, you forget [them . . .]. And when some law gets passed by accident that might hamper capital, you forget that! You forgot the Sherman [anti-Trust] Act till some of you figured out how you could apply it to the Labour Unions!' Capraro evaded the draft because the First World War 'was a war for business, a war for billions of dollars, murder of young men for billions'. While the play's treatment of rebels as heroes generates exciting drama, particularly in their defiant dialogue under cross-examination in court, it undermines rebelliousness. The characters are so clearly virtuous or villainous that much of the play lacks credibility. Suvorin, the character derived from Madeiros, is father of Macready's sweetheart, a sentimentalisation of the issues. His pessimism concerning the efficacy of radicalism subverts what the condemned men represent. He calls socialists, anarchists and wobblies 'fools' for wanting to change the government since those who own it 'will buy any government you have'.

As the title *Elizabeth the Queen* (1930) hints, Elizabeth I is a queen first, a woman in love necessarily second if she is to remain queen. As she foresees, the rivals of her lover Essex goad him into leading an expedition to put down a rebellion in Ireland. Taking advantage of his absence, they intercept his and Elizabeth's letters to each other, thus breeding rebellion in him, suspicion of treason in her. The only letter he receives from her orders him to disband his army and return to her alone. Refusing to disband, he arrives to seize the kingdom. Rising to the occasion, Elizabeth reveals herself to be the more politically adroit. Alone, they perceive what happened to their letters, but if he had no rebellious thoughts, she points out, he would not have come with an army to make her his prisoner, which she is. Refusing to surrender power, she offers to share it with him if he disbands his army. Expecting marriage, he does so. She then tells him that to rule one must be 'friendless, without mercy, without love', orders him to be arrested and taken to the Tower. Earlier, she gave him a ring which, were he to send it to her, would gain her forgiveness. He refuses to do so, she refuses to pardon him unless he does so. Anderson undercuts their stature. Sending for Essex, she takes 'the first step', a compromise a tragic hero does not make. Admitting he loves her, he refuses to give her the ring, for he knows that if he is pardoned he will try to depose her. Although the dramatic intent may be to demonstrate integrity, the effect is sentimentality, which diminishes his stature. 'Give me the ring', she pleads, 'I'd rather you killed me/Than I killed you': a reversal of her former stance, which lowers her stature. He prefers to die rather than rule less well then he knows she would: an admission that lowers his stature. Next, exit her tragic stature as she cries, 'Take my kingdom. It is yours!' Instead of an unyielding battle for a throne, he goes to his death renouncing what he claimed to have wanted and she humiliates herself to no avail. Potentially the play is a tragedy along Hegelian lines, but instead of incompatible forces, power and love, making mutually exclusive demands on a queen and an earl as each totally submits to one of them, Elizabeth and Essex equivocate. He gets neither love nor throne; she gets the throne by default. But while the play fails as tragedy it succeeds as a non-tragic conflict. Why must one take the position that if a play is not a tragedy it is a poor play? Why must one accept the author's intention as guide? *Elizabeth the Queen* falls short of Anderson's aspirations but succeeds as non-tragic drama.

In *Night Over Taos* (1932) Anderson tries to establish the tragic stature of Pablo Montoya, aristocratic leader of the Spaniards in Taos, New Mexico, which in 1847 America wanted to annex. He has a tragic flaw: 'His father was lord of life and death before him, and he's been a god so long here in the valley that he thinks he's a god in fact. That's his strength, too, though it sometimes makes him a fool.' Folly, not strength, emerges. Challenged by a new way of life, represented by America, he becomes a stubborn, vindictive old man. Since he and his sons want to marry an American, Diana, the thematic intent is that the

1. Dudley Digges in the dock in *The Adding Machine* by Elmer Rice, setting by Lee Simonson, New York 1923

2. Dudley Digges and the giant adding machine in *The Adding Machine*. Setting by Lee Simonson, New York 1923

3. *Street Scene* by Elmer Rice, with the Jo Mielziner set, New York 1929

4. *You Can't Take it with you* by George Kaufman and Moss Hart, New York 1936, with Josephine Hull (*right*), George Tobias (*left*), and Henry Travers (*with hand on chair*)

5. *Winterset* by Maxwell Anderson, with the Jo Mielziner set, New York 1935, with Eduardo Cianelli (*second from left*) and Burgess Meredith and Margo (*right*)

6. *Waiting for Lefty* by Clifford Odets, with Elia Kazan in the foreground, New York 1935

7. *Awake and Sing* by Clifford Odets. *Left to right:* John Garfield, Morris Carnovsky, J. Edward Bromberg, Stella Adler, Luther Adler, Sanford Meisner, Art Smith. New York 1935

8. *Our Town* by Thornton Wilder, New York 1938, with Martha Scott standing in white dress

9. *The Skin of our Teeth* by Thornton Wilder, New York 1942. *Left to right:* Montgomery Clift, Frederich March and Florence Eldridge

10. *The Little Foxes* by Lillian Hellman. *Left to right:* Lee Baker, Tallulah Bankhead, Carl Benton Reid, Dan Duryea, Charles Dingle. New York 1939

11. *The Time of Your Life* by William Saroyan, with Julie Haydon seated in centre, Gene Kelly dancing and Eddie Dowling seated right. New York 1939

seeds of the old order's destruction lie within it. After Montoya has killed his older son for treason, a love triangle develops between him, Diana and his younger son, whom she loves. Warned that as the way of nature is for youth to want youth he should relinquish his right under the old order to marry Diana, he finally submits, but then poisons himself – a stale theatrical gesture. Anderson trivialises social themes by a romantic story: a propensity to which he often succumbs. He thereby de-emphasises an important subject: whether to grant the masses a little power to prevent them from taking more. Because neighbouring Mexico and the United States are republics that have broken from their kings, a priest tells Montoya, peons, have begun to wonder why in Taos 'one class of men,/Or one man out of that class, has it all his own way'. To save the aristocracy, the priest would 'seem to offer them from within/What's offered from outside', such as schools and the franchise, would 'give them the shadow/Or they'll want the substance'. To Montoya, such ideas will lead to the peons' wanting a republic. Since modern audiences are unlikely to regard what he represents as noble, this theme undermines his stature.

Potentially a suitable tragic hero is the title character of *Mary of Scotland* (1934), whose charm and integrity Anderson dramatises. He also dramatises the political skills of her antagonist, Elizabeth I of England. Since Mary is in Scotland against Elizabeth's wishes, has been crowned against her policy, is Catholic thus dangerous to her Protestant reign, is next heir to the throne that some believe is occupied by a bastard, Elizabeth elects to destroy Mary, whose reign makes hers insecure. Because Mary wants an heir, which Elizabeth does not have, Elizabeth contrives to have her persuaded to marry Darnley, a fool who would ruin her and a Catholic who would alienate further the Protestant half of her subjects. When Mary does so, though she loves Bothwell, she proves herself Elizabeth's 'puppet'. After Darnley's murder, Elizabeth manoeuvres her into marrying Bothwell, while she plants suspicion that Bothwell killed Darnley with Mary's help. Again Anderson dramatises Elizabeth's capacities to rule and Mary's incapacities. When Mary, Elizabeth's prisoner, meets her (historically she did not), Mary blames herself for having failed to perceive her rival's machinations. Elizabeth tells her she has no hope of rescue but Mary prefers prison to abdication. To her, and evidently to Anderson who concludes the play with her triumph, Mary ultimately wins, for 'I have loved as a woman loves,/Lost as a woman loses. I have a son,/And he will rule Scotland – and England. You have no heir!' Yet despite Mary's humanity and defiance, she wanted to rule Scotland but was overthrown and wanted to love her lover but was separated from him. Consistently outwitted by her antagonist, she fails as tragic hero and becomes a pitiful loser. While *Mary of Scotland* is not the tragedy Anderson would have, it is a powerful study of a naïve political idealist versus a calculating political realist.

Wingless Victory (1936), which also fails as tragedy, has nothing to compensate. How can one take seriously a play that begins on a wintry night in Salem in 1800, with a minister spitting in the face of a shawled girl who carries a baby in her arms, as he drives her outside, though the child might die? This hackneyed melodramatic start heralds most moments of the play, in which New Englanders welcome the money of a prodigal son who – when slavery existed – expects them also to welcome his Malaysian wife and child. As anyone with sense might have anticipated, they take his money and order her out, allowing him to go or stay as he pleases. That she kills her children as Medea does, and herself as Medea does not, is insufficient to make the play tragic, or good.

High Tor (1937), also in verse, does not aim at tragedy. Van Van Dorn, who scorns traditional values, does not want to sell the titular mountain because real estate developers would ruin its beauty. Since he needs only the amount of money he can earn in three weeks, he works no longer and spends the rest of his time hunting and fishing. An individualist, he is among the last of a dying breed, like the Indian he promises to bury, and almost a ghost, like Henry Hudson's crew which populates the mountain. Opposed to him are thieving land developers, who resemble armed robbers, also present on High Tor. Recognising that all ways of life change – his, Van's and the businessmen's – the Indian advises Van to sell: no hill is worth one's peace of mind.

Key Largo treats this question, whether to battle powerful forces, as tragedy. In Spain near the end of its Civil War (March 1939, eight months before the play opened) are remnants of a squad of the Abraham Lincoln Brigade (American volunteers for the Loyalists, who fought Franco's fascists). Because there is no point in dying for a cause that is both lost and corrupted (the communists control the anti-fascist forces), McCloud wants to desert. Victor's reasons for remaining persuade the others to join him. He must believe that something in the world, a force for good, 'would rather die than accept injustice [. . .] or I'll die inside'. In the long run, this something would defeat the Hitlers and Mussolinis (Franco's allies). By staying he keeps faith: 'In myself and what men are./ And in what we may be.' After they have died, McCloud visits their families to seek forgiveness for having survived by working with Franco's army, which captured him. He comes to Victor's father and sister in the Florida key that gives the play its title and suggests its scope. Gangsters led by Murillo, who runs a rigged roulette wheel, occupy their home. As parallel to the fascists, Murillo is nicknamed Mussolini. When he demands that McCloud return thirty dollars he won at gambling (an inducement to bet more), they point guns at each other. McCloud backs down. At the play's end, however, when two innocent Indians might be arrested for a murder Murillo has committed, he takes a stand: confessing so that the Indians may flee, he then uses a gun to hold the law at bay while he prepares to kill Murillo, which he does but not until after one of the mob has shot him.

Among the deficiencies of *Key Largo*, McCloud's final recognition that 'a man must die for what he believes' or his life will be death is little different from Victor's belief and not expressed as well. *Key Largo* takes a long while to arrive where it started. Furthermore, the characters ask the wrong question. McCloud is right to desert. Despite Victor's moving argument, the cause is lost and death is certain. The real issue is not *whether* but *under what circumstances* one might die for a cause. McCloud is right not to risk his life for thirty dollars, equally right to risk it when he can save innocent men and kill a gangster. In *The Eve of St. Mark* Americans on a small Philippine island face Japanese troops. They must choose 'whether we'll let ourselves be driven back – or hang on here. But if we do hang on – I doubt if we'll all live. I doubt if any of us will. [. . .] We're not ordered to stay here. It's only – that we're needed, and we know it.' The point is *that we're needed*. In April 1942, four months after Japan had bombed Pearl Harbor and propelled America into the Second World War, Americans were ill-prepared for war. Unlike the last weeks of the Spanish Civil War, ultimate defeat was not certain. The need for time for America to consolidate its

strength sufficiently to help defeat the Axis powers vali-
dated the risk of one's life. For *The Eve of St. Mark* to pose
the correct question does not suffice to make the play good,
but for *Key Largo* to pose an incorrect one helps to weaken
it.

Anderson also dramatises the established order his
individualists defy. *Knickerbocker Holiday* (1938) defines a
quintessential American as one with an 'aversion to taking
orders', an 'abhorrence of governmental corruption', and
an 'incapacity for doing anything about it'. Its preface
states, 'the gravest and most constant danger to a man's life,
liberty, and happiness is the government under which he
lives'. Anderson distrusts government as a gangsterlike
business with 'plundering, buttered over at the top by a
hypocritical pretense at patriotic unselfishness'. A
government-dominated economy can only result in 'a loss
of individual liberty in thought, speech, and action'
(pp. 82–3). He is wary of governmental restrictions too far
beyond traffic regulations.

Punning on a phrase in *Romeo and Juliet*, 'A plague o'
both your houses', *Both your Houses* (1933) refers to
America's bicameral legislature. The theme recalls another
pun, Will Rogers' remark that America has the best
politicians money can buy – though both have faith that one
day the electorate will, in the slang of the period, get wise to
the bums and kick them out of office. A freshman
Congressman discovers that an appropriation bill is
inflated because of pork barrel riders (amendments with
appropriations for other projects, giving congressmen pat-
ronage powers to benefit themselves, special interest
groups, and constituents). Unable to defeat it directly, he
tries to do so indirectly: adding more riders to make the bill
so bloated that no one would dare vote for it. But by giving
every interest group what it wants he eliminates all

opposition. Expressions of disillusionment are usually comic, for instance, 'the sole business of government is graft, special privilege and corruption – with a byproduct of order. They have to keep order or they can't make collections.' As Anderson states in *Valley Forge* (1934), such government goes back to the Revolution: 'This war began to protect our trade. The merchants/were being run out of business by subsidies/to English boats.' They wanted 'profits, not freedom'. In *Knickerbocker Holiday*, about the Dutch when New York City was called New Amsterdam, Anderson says the same. Pieter Stuyvesant defines government as 'a group of men organised to sell protection to the inhabitants of a limited area – at monopolized prices'. This comedy (with music by Kurt Weill) ends reassuringly: 'I guess all governments are crooked, I guess they're all vicious and corrupt, but a democracy has the immense advantage of being incompetent in villainy and clumsy in corruption'. In a serious vein, a policeman in *Key Largo* utters similar sentiments: in politics 'what you have to do is sell protection/to people that can pay' and 'I've heard it said/there's honest government somewhere, here and there,/by fits and starts. Maybe there is. I don't know./I don't see how it could last.'

The *Masque of Kings* (1937) unsuccessfully combines themes of autocracy, rebellion and democracy in an effort at poetic tragedy. In Vienna in 1889, Crown Prince Rudolph wants to free Hungary from the Austrian Empire. He refuses to reign as his father has but would give Hungary autonomy, extend the franchise, establish free speech and press, and give parliament power. When the opportunity arises, he sees that to free Hungary he must force his father to abdicate and to realise his goals he must kill opponents, censor the press, 'guard the trough/for those whose feet are in it', and rule as ruthlessly as his father. To avoid becoming what he hates, he withdraws from the arena, ending the rebellion. Anderson's implications are perniciously counter-revolutionary. Why try to improve society since the result is foredoomed? One either leaves conditions as bad as they are or creates conditions just as bad. The protagonist's spinelessness disqualifies him from the role of tragic hero. Worsening the play is a romance that adds a dramatically irrelevant third act. When Rudolph learns that his mistress initially reported their meetings to his father, he becomes disillusioned. The lovers commit suicide. The political ideas harmonise with those of Anderson's other plays. In *The Star-Wagon* (1937) Stephen invents a machine that takes him back thirty-five years. When he returns he says that neither his machine nor anything else can change the world or the people in it: an echo of the futilitarian theme of *Masque of Kings*.

Joan of Lorraine (written 1944, produced 1946) poses a related question. Should one deal with corrupt people to accomplish good, which may only be minimal? Employing a play within a play, Anderson has characters compare compromise to get a Joan of Arc play produced with the situation of Joan, who is asked to compromise with corrupt courtiers and Dauphin. When the actress playing Joan complains the inner play means that 'we all have to compromise and work with evil men – and that if you have a faith it will come to nothing unless you get some of the forces of evil on your side', the director responds, 'You'll touch dishonesty somewhere as soon as you start to get anything done!' But she recognises that Joan's integrity 'will always come through, and all the rest will be forgotten' – repudiating Stephen's view in *The Star-Wagon*, 'The world's made up of crooks and thieves, and if you want to do business and eat regular meals you have to be one of them!'

Anderson's most notable effort, like W. B. Yeats' before

him, was to create a renaissance in poetic drama. Ibsen defended his decision to write prose on the ground that verse would have counteracted realism. 'We are no longer living in the days of Shakespeare' and today's human beings do not 'talk "the language of the Gods"'. He predicted: 'It is improbable that verse will be employed to any extent worth mentioning in the drama of the immediate future; the aims of the dramatists of the future are almost certain to be incompatible with it. It is therefore doomed.'[2] Wrong, according to Anderson, who wanted the theatre to have a higher literary quality than it did. He maintained that prose was the language of 'journalistic social comment' and only 'occasionally' reached 'the upper air of poetic tragedy' (p. 48). Unfortunately, his verse is unconfined to the upper air, for example, 'What do you hear?'/'The breathing of our guest –/a man sleeping lightly. – His face is toward the wall/by the way the sound comes to me' (*Key Largo*) and 'This is the question –/do we make a try for H 25 and home/or man the gun while we can, fire the few shells,/sink the invasion barges, never let them in/till they've paid the last death' (*Eve of St. Mark*). Even the echo of *Hamlet* in the second quotation does not elevate the language.

A problem with Anderson's verse, says Alan R. Thompson so ably that I can only quote him,[3] is its 'slight' metre. Verse is distinguishable from prose 'only by having a recognizable prosodic pattern, but the nearest approach to such a pattern that I can discover [. . .] is a blank verse so much less regular than Shakespeare's at his freest that if it were written in solid prose form a reader could never guess that it was intended to be verse, still less where each line (except the first) should begin.' He refers to *Winterset*. Since I will be discussing *Winterset* later, here is an example from *Mary of Scotland*:

It's dangerous to be honest with you, my Bothwell, but
honest I'll be. Since I've been woman grown there's been
no man save you but I could take his hand steadily in
mine, and look in his eyes steadily, too, and feel in myself
more power than I felt in him. All but yourself. There is
aching fire between us, fire that could take deep hold and
burn down all the marshes of the west and make us great
or slay us.

'Split this into phrases', as Thompson says of his example,
'and each one is rhythmical by itself, perhaps; at least, it
sounds well when delivered eloquently, which I think is
what most people who talk of "prose rhythm" really mean.
But it has no metre.' Neither Thompson nor I overlook the
effectiveness of such passages when actors deliver them
well, but 'whatever rhythmical effects [they have] are
discontinuous and irregular, and [. . .] therefore they are
not, in any exact sense, verse effects'. Apropos, the *New
York Times'* review of the first production of *Elizabeth the
Queen*, which was written in verse, praised Anderson's
'prose that has pith and resiliency'.

According to Anderson poetry is 'the language of
emotion' (p. 50). But his is inflated. In *Valley Force*, for
example, Lafayette's rhetoric is windy ('Lose! Now the
gods/in heaven hear me, you cannot lose!' is a small part)
and Washington's imagery is pretentious ('The spirit of
earth/moves over the earth like flame and finds fresh/home
when the old's burned out' is a small part). As George Jean
Nathan observes of *The Masque of Kings*, when the
Emperor asks 'that you state briefly/what meaning you
may wish me to attach to these hot cries from your heart?'
Rudolph replies with nineteen lines 'answering almost
everything but the questions asked' and when an Archduke
declares, 'Back through recorded time/no prince was ever

offered such a kingdom/on such a platter', Rudolph 'proceeds promptly to exile drama into the wings with exactly thirty-four lines of broken verse setting forth his views on Alexander the Great, Napoleon, the fateful drift of the Austrian empire, the inauguration of necessary reforms, the danger of war, the tragedies of absolutism, his future policies and the futility of the war dead'.[4] As these examples demonstrate, Anderson's poetry often diverges from his drama. Recall T. S. Eliot's perception: Shakespeare's poetry 'never interrupts the action, or is out of character, but on the contrary, in some mysterious way supports both action and character'. Poetry that is dramatic 'does not interrupt but intensifies the dramatic situation'.[5]

Anderson wants both elevation and colloquialism. In all likelihood, no one unfamiliar with the plays would guess the sources of 'If you draw that pistol I'll put a slug through your pump' and 'He's a punk,/And he'll rule like a punk!' They are 'poetic' lines from *Valley Force* and *Mary of Scotland*. The slang jars and the incongruity of words and period is laughable.

'Winterset'

Like *Gods of the Lightning*, *Winterset* (1935) derives from the Sacco–Vanzetti case. According to Anderson, its genesis was a statement by Robert H. Montgomery, who in 1960 would write *Sacco–Vanzetti: The Murder and the Myth*. Montgomery told Anderson not to think badly of the judge who condemned them for 'the poor old fellow [. . .] was just about out of his mind. He went around asking one man after another, "What was wrong about that? They were guilty. They were obviously guilty. I had to do this and this and this – legally I was in a box. I had to do it. They were

– the evidence was such that I really couldn't do anything else." Montgomery said, "The old fellow really deserves your sympathy." "[6] Unlike *Gods of the Lightning, Winterset* takes place years after the execution. A professor has written an article claiming that a key witness, Garth Esdras, was not called to testify. Seeking to clear his father's name, Mio Romagna (Mio is short for Bartolomeo, Vanzetti's given name) comes to New York to find him. So does the gangster Trock Estrella, newly released from jail, to ensure Garth's silence, since Trock led the gang and may have committed the murder. So too does Judge Gaunt, now old and insane, to learn whether he had been right. Mio discovers his father's innocence, falls in love with Garth's sister Miriamne, and with her is killed by Trock's henchmen.

The first verse tragedy in a contemporary setting to be produced on Broadway, where it was a box-office success, *Winterset* deliberately resonates Shakespearean themes: a son out to avenge his father (*Hamlet*), a mock trial during a storm (*King Lear*), a teenage boy and girl falling in love at a dance (*Romeo and Juliet*, and his nickname recalls Romeo). As one critic perceives:

it appears to be Anderson's intention that the Shakespearean parallels will actually *force* the audience to respond to the characters in specific ways, whether emotionally or intellectually; and because of the vigourous explicitness of the allusions, the responses are intended to be immediate and powerful. [. . .] To recall Hamlet in Mio compels one to *respond* to Mio as he has to respond to Hamlet, not merely to see the parallel of sons avenging their fathers' deaths, but to react emotionally to the modern avenger as one has previously reacted to Shakespeare's.[7]

Although I find nothing compelling about such response and reaction, I agree as to Anderson's intention.

Amidst drab contemporaneity, Anderson provides visual spectacle. A gangster, Shadow, whom Trock's men riddle with bullets and throw into the river, returns dripping and bleeding, gun in hand, to avenge himself. Referring to his father, Mio makes the thematic link: 'Romagna was dead, too, and Shadow was dead, but the time's come when you can't keep them down, these dead men!' In a lively scene, a character plays a hurdy gurdy (a street piano on wheels, hauled like a pushcart, operated by turning a handle) and assorted waterfront types dance – only to be stopped by a policeman who enforces a mayoral edict against music in the streets. The spectacle serves several purposes: it enables Mio and Miriamne to meet in a romantic manner; it enlivens an otherwise gloomy atmosphere; it demonstrates the law's adversarial treatment of the lower classes, stopping the dance and trying to arrest a radical for making a speech – present action suggestive of what happened to Mio's father; it dramatises Mio's stature and intellect when he publicly mocks an initially uncomprehending policeman.

And the exterior set is '*the bank of a river under a bridgehead*' whose span is '*gigantic*'. As realised by Jo Mielziner, it had 'remote majesty' (*New York Times*) and 'soaring beauty' (*New York Sun*). As Joseph Wood Krutch describes (*Nation*) and photographs confirm, it was 'breathtaking':

> To the right the huge concrete pier of a bridge lifts itself sheer into the darkness above, and to the left a sullen block of tenements balances the opposing mass. In the remote gloom of these lower depths the solid foundation of the proud bridge equates itself with the dismal despair

of the tenements, and the fact adds meaning to the pure plastic beauty of the forms. Physically and spiritually the foundations upon which the city rests are seen from the perspective of those who crawl around their bases, and it is not often that the creative possibilities of stage designs have been so convincingly demonstrated.

Ultimately, however, a poetic tragedy stands or falls on the bases of poetry and tragedy. On both, *Winterset* falls.

Anderson often uses poetry for non-elevated subjects. Garth says, 'You're a bright girl, sis. – /You see too much. You run along and cook./Why don't you go to school?' Not only does metric verse do nothing that prose cannot do, but the actor who plays Garth has an insoluble problem, since a dramatist who alternates poetry and prose implicitly demands different delivery for each (else why write differently?). If the actor speaks these lines as realism (which they are), the audience is unaware they are verse. If he speaks them to reveal their metric regularity, he sounds pretentious.

When Anderson's verse employs slang, the tonal clash with elevated speech is ludicrously incongruous. A gangster says, 'give me leave/to kid a little'. Gangster or not, when one wants to kid a little one does not ask leave to do so. Instead of dignifying the character, such language mocks the attempt at dignity. The secret of the play's success is the actors. Take part of Trock's first speech: 'You roost of punks and gulls! Sleep it off,/whatever you had last night, get down in warm,/one big ham-fat against another – sleep,/cling, sleep and rot! Rot out your pasty guts/with diddling, you had no brains to begin.' On the page a gangster versifying about punks, sleeping it off, pasty guts, and diddling is preposterous. While most actors would draw unintentional laughter, the first actor who spoke these lines, and who recreated the role in the 1939 film, became famous on the screen for his villainous characters: Eduardo Ciannelli whose scowling face and raspy voice are fearful. The actor who in the film *Gunga Din* snarlingly commanded his followers to kill for Kali and for the love of killing without provoking laughter delivered this speech to no giggles or titters. Reviewers were mesmerised by his vigorous portrait of malevolence' (*New York Times*), which 'casts a spell of evil' (*Newsweek*). To those familiar with his films, the invocation of his name creates in the mind's ear his rendering of that passage. When he tells his henchman, 'laugh at somebody else!/it's a lot safer!' spectators too obey.

Anderson cleverly persuades us to accept 17-year-old Mio as a verse speaker. Early, he has Mio quip on the first stanza of Tennyson's *Sir Galahad* ('My strength is as the strength of ten,/Because my heart is pure'):

MIO: [. . .] Maybe I stank, too, but a hobo has the stench of ten because his shoes are poor.
CARR: Tennyson.
MIO: Right. Jeez, I'm glad we met up again! Never knew anybody else that could track me through the driven snow of Victorian literature.
CARR: Now you're cribbing from some half-forgotten criticism of Ben Jonson's Roman plagiarisms.

While I have entirely forgotten the second allusion, if in fact I ever knew it, this dialogue establishes Mio's literary and linguistic skills. In other ways as well, Anderson calls attention to them: at the dance, the policeman calls him 'professor'; he attended secondary school though it was not compulsory (when discovered to be a non-resident whose family did not pay taxes, he was expelled); and he spent

96

New York winters in the large public library near Times Square. Thus, Mio's verse, often with literary allusions, seems realistic – particularly with Burgess Meredith as Mio. When one imagines him speaking such passages as the one that gives the play its title

> Now all you silent powers
> that make the sleet and dark, and never yet
> have spoken, give us a sign, let the throw be ours
> this once, on this longest night, when the winter sets
> his foot on the threshold leading up to spring
> and enters with remembered cold – let fall
> some mercy with the rain. We are two lovers
> here in your night, and we wish to live.

one can overlook the irregular metre of half the lines, the pretentious invocation, and the absurd imagery (when winter enters, cold is present, not remembered), for the actor provides the impact that the poet lacks. Critics praised Meredith's 'astonishingly agile emotionalism', 'febrile force and inspired precision' (*Brooklyn Daily Eagle*) that put a 'solid foundation' to the play (*New York Times*).

Anderson's verse is windy and poor. In Mio's statement that when he first saw Miriamne 'I heard myself saying,/this is a face that launches ships for me – /and if I owned a dream – yes, half a dream –/we'd share it', the self-conscious allusion to Marlow's *Faustus* undermines the appropriate image that follows. Neither does it help that the entire speech occupies a full page. Moreover, many of the play's poetic passages do not intensify but interrupt the dramatic momentum to become spoken arias, such as Esdras' thirty-one-line sermon on guiltlessness, with such pompous phrases as 'what is seen is traced in air' and 'Let the wind and fire take that hour to ashes'.

How did the film cope with Anderson's poetry? Simple: it cut a great deal of it, 'sometimes with happy results', for you are not 'asked to hold your breath through the interminable lovemaking between Mio and Miriamne while gangsters wait to kill them' (*New York Herald Tribune*). For that matter, part of the impact of the first stage production may derive from the same practice. In the text the play's final speech, Esdras' oration over the bodies of Mio and Miriamne, has thirty lines. Sensibly, Anderson permitted director Guthrie McClintic to cut all but the first twelve and a half lines.[8]

As tragedy, *Winterset* is muddled. At the start, Mio is an embittered outcast on the far side of despair, aiming to find evidence to clear his father's name despite the probability that authorities would suppress it. Anderson helps to create credibility for the mutual attraction of Mio and Miriamne by making her Jewish, therefore also outside conventional American society and endangered, particularly in 1935, two years after Hitler had become Chancellor of Germany and long after he had begun to boycott, ostracise and terrorise Jews. America was then rife with anti-semitism. When Miriamne says, 'my people are Jews', Mio immediately responds, and audiences understood, 'Then you know something about it'. When he learns the truth, he vows to publicise it, although Judge Gaunt pleads that to do so would harm the common good by undermining the state. In the last act Mio changes his mind. 'I've lost/my taste for revenge if it falls on you', he tells Miriamne, who consoles him on the basis that his father 'would have forgiven'. Some condemn the play as tragedy because this reversal represents a compromise with radical ideas and an unbelievable alteration of a lifetime purpose through the love-at-first-sight of a girl he met that very day. I think *Winterset* fails for a different reason. Although it seems plausible that love would make Mio abandon a goal that would hurt his beloved, he does not embrace a higher ethic as such, the abjuration of vengeance, which might be tragically ennobling, not merely romantic. If he did, Anderson might have linked his title, based on the winter solstice, to an anniversary that closely follows, Christmas. But note that the moral he has Esdras draw is not the abandonment of revenge. Rather: 'this is the glory of earth-born men and women/not to cringe, never to yield, but standing,/take defeat implacable and defiant,/die unsubmitting'. The statement is specious for, as Eleanor Flexner observes, '*to submit* is exactly what Mio did'.[9]

Reviewers may tend to accept a serious verse play as tragic if the hero dies at the end. In contrast to *Hamlet*, whose hero's 'inky cloak' and 'customary suits of solemn black' presage his death from the first act, death does not inhere in *Winterset*. I dispute Flexner's suggestion that Mio might jump into the East River to swim away from Trock's killers (the wintry night is too cold for that), but I agree that he might shoot his gun to attract the police (if a hurdy gurdy brings one in Act I, a pistol shot might do so in Act III) or ask his friend Carr, who enters and leaves the area without interference, to get help – which Carr offers to do but Mio refuses. Because in 1939 the screen Production Code Administration prevented evil from defeating good, the film let Mio and Miriamne live. Reviewing an off-Broadway revival of the play in 1966, Stanley Kaufmann (*New York Times*) notes, 'The flimsiness of the catastrophe is underscored by memory of the happy ending of the film version' in which Mio wheels out the hurdy gurdy that is stored in a nearby shed, thus bringing irate police who 'take him and the girl – safely – to jail. A mark of this tragedy's lack of conviction is that I kept wondering why the hero in this production wasn't as bright as the one in the movie.' Although a happy end might have improved *Winterset* somewhat, it would still be a muddled tragedy.

In this review Kaufman calls Anderson 'a man who very much wanted to achieve poetic tragedy but whose main qualification was earnestness'. Whatever the virtues of *Elizabeth the Queen* and *Mary of Scotland*, that judgment stands. Ibsen's view that poetic tragedy is no longer feasible has yet to be disproved.

6
Clifford Odets

In the early 1930s workers' theatre groups proliferated. *New Theatre* magazine, which started in 1934, sponsored benefit performances of short plays and dances at a theatre near Union Square, New York. On the benefit night of 6 January 1935 Clifford Odets presented *Waiting for Lefty*, where the situation is a taxi union meeting called to decide whether to strike. On stage are Fatt, a crooked union leader, his gunman, and the strike committee, who await the arrival of another leader, Lefty. Planted with us in the audience are cabbies. As members of the committee and someone chosen by Fatt directly address the cabbies (and us), Odets dramatises in flashbacks what led to the meeting. The issues involve more than low wages and embrace a social spectrum that includes industry, government and medicine. Joe's wife Edna persuades him to strike because they cannot properly feed their children, buy sufficient clothing, or pay rent. Refusing an industrialist's offer to help make poison gas for the government and to inform on a scientist, a lab assistant quits to become a cabby. Irv tries to persuade his sister Florence not to marry her boy friend Sid, a hack who earns too little to support a family (they would move back with him and his mother, an added mouth for Irv to feed); Sid agrees; a strike for higher wages would help them to live humanly. A supposed taxi driver brought onstage by Fatt is exposed by a cabby in the audience as a labour spy, hired by the company. To economise, a hospital's Board of Directors closes the charity ward and fires its personnel, including a Jewish interne sacked because of anti-semitism even though he has seniority over an incompetent man; despite Jews on the Board, there 'doesn't seem to be much difference between wealthy Jews and rich Gentiles'. When the Jew complains, 'Doctors don't run medicine in this country', Odets implies that workers and not capitalists should be in charge. The interne becomes a cabby. A driver urges the union members in the audience not to wait for Lefty but to act on their own, which is to say that no single leader is indispensable and the workers should decide collectively.[1] Learning that Lefty has been murdered, he urges the cabbies to vote to strike, which they do. *Waiting for Lefty* is not a drama of ideas but an agitprop play: it agitates and propagandises to secure an emotional rather than an intellectual response. Genuine members of its first audience yelled 'Strike!' together with the planted actors. All were carried along by emotions that brought them together in rare unity.

Everyone who has recorded that performance was aware of its unexpected momentousness. *Lefty* immediately became the play of the day, Odets the man of the moment. Within weeks labour and left-wing theatres throughout the country sought to perform it. Censors tried to prevent production on grounds of subversion, obscenity and blasphemy: sometimes they succeeded. In March *Lefty* moved to Broadway. It is significant of its impact that several reviewers proclaimed that no matter whether one agreed, disagreed or was indifferent about Odets' views one should see the play for its dramatic originality, emotional power and contemporaneity. With *Lefty* radical drama, previously on the fringe of American theatre, entered the mainstream.

Odets wrote his first six plays, on which his reputation rests, in the 1930s, during the Depression, when unemployment topped sixteen million, when breadlines formed on Times Square, when the name of President Franklin D. Roosevelt's predecessor was used to describe shantytowns of cardboard or tin houses (Hoovervilles) and empty pockets (Hoover dollars). Although Odets' plays reflect these desperate realities, they are infrequently straightforward propaganda pieces. Anyone in search of a coherent political or economic programme looks in vain, finding more ambiguity than he expects. *Lefty* ends with a call to strike, not to join the Communist Party. Anti-Nazi German communists are the heroes of *Till the Day I Die* (1935), a one-acter written to be performed with *Lefty* for a full evening, but they are the exception and not the rule. In his other plays, which are full-length, the only professional labour organiser, Frank in *Golden Boy* (1937), works for the CIO (Congress of Industrial Organisations), which is not communist. Only for a brief period of time was Odets himself a Party member.

One need not be a communist or a socialist to deplore a system that creates mass unemployment, with its attendant sufferings. In an appendix to the Modern Library edition of Odets' *Six Plays*, Harold Clurman calls Odets 'a poet of the decaying middle class with revolutionary yearnings and convictions'. From the tension between these yearnings and his class's ideals come desires to reject false values and to realise one's potentials in a full life. Except for the cardboard villains of his one-act plays, Odets seems to love his characters. He sympathises with their weaknesses, deplores their need to compromise with reality, pleads for lives with dignity. His revolutionism, more emotional than ideological, derives as much from youthful fervour (he was under 30 when he wrote his first four plays) as from a view of an economic system that destroys people and crushes the human spirit.

Politico-economic considerations are prominent in almost all his plays. 'Till the day we die there is steady work to do', destroying the Nazis, says a character who explains the title of that play. In this uncomplicated drama Nazis capture a communist, torture him, and make him seem a turncoat; to avoid trapping his colleagues he kills himself. Though hackneyed, the play demonstrates one of Odets' virtues, characterisation: a terrified Jewish German, married to a Nordic woman, for a time passes himself off as an Aryan Nazi.

Characterisation is also among the chief appeals of *Paradise Lost* (1935), whose title indicates its theme, the loss of what the middle class considers paradise. As exemplified in dialogue between Sam Katz and Gus, money is this class's linchpin: 'Excuse me, please, keep quiet'. 'No, I won't, I ain't your servant.' 'You got the five dollars you owe me?' 'No.' 'So keep quiet. (GUS *is cowed.*)' Like thousands of businesses at the time, that of Katz and Leo Gordon is bankrupt: in fact and symbol. Confronted by a workers' delegation, Gordon learns that Katz exploits them. While Katz pleads that the firm cannot remain solvent unless he does so, Gordon insists 'it's wrong. I would not want my life built up on the misery of these people. [. . .] What is to be done?' Since another character emphasises '(*portentously*) That is the question – "What is to be done?"' Odets may allude to the title of a famous pamphlet by Lenin, but Gordon's answer is not revolution: 'our workers must have better conditions!' Impotent to avoid economic collapse, Katz is also sexually impotent. Though Gordon is procreative, he too is unable to save his business or his children. Economically and domestically, the middle class collapses. A son who studies the stock market slowly dies of sleeping sickness – symbolism that may seem stale on page but is moving on stage. When another son, Ben, a former Olympic athlete, marries but cannot find a job he joins his friend Kewpie in a robbery; upon learning that Kewpie had an affair with his wife he virtually commits suicide when apprehended: a winner of medals for running, he merely stands to be shot. The daughter, a pianist, does not marry because neither she nor her boy friend can earn a living. She wastes away, losing him (to another city, where he seeks work) and her piano (to creditors). One representative of business is impotent; another sires dying representatives of finance, sport and art. But their complex humanity, not what they symbolise, dominates. Kewpie, for instance, envies and truly loves Ben; and when the Gordons are dispossessed Leo and his wife affectionately kiss each other.

Economics and action fuse in *Golden Boy*, whose title character, Joe Bonaparte, about to turn 21, chooses between a career as a violinist or as a boxer. At the start he has not mastered either: he has won a scholarship to a major music school and though able in the ring has not fought professionally. The fiddle contends with the fist, non-commercial with commercial. Depression America governs his choice of which potential to develop. As the Jewish friend of Joe's father asks, 'could a boy make a living playing this instrument in our competitive civilisation today?' Joe wishes he lived 'where poverty's no shame', 'where there's no war in the streets'. The title points to

Joe's success in the ring and to society's standard for success. Money means life with dignity. But money corrupts. One antithesis is the fist and the fiddle; another is Fuselli, a killer and gangster whose rackets include prizefighting, and Joe's father, who represents old-fashioned virtues. Another option is Joe's brother Frank. 'I fight', he says – but as a CIO organiser in behalf of workers; he gains satisfaction, not wealth.

Once Joe chooses the fist his downfall is inevitable, for he becomes part of a system in which human beings are commodities. The boxing world employs such terms as: 'I bought a piece of him'. Although he complains that his promoter Moody 'treats me like a possession', he tells Moody's mistress Lorna he wishes 'you belonged to me', showing that he considers her a possession. When he defeats another boxer to become eligible for the title bout his success sours: he accidentally kills his opponent in the ring. What gives Joe stature is that despite his intention he accepts responsibility: 'I didn't mean it! [. . .] But I *did* it!' His subsequent death with Lorna in an expensive automobile (the reward and symbol of his career choice), perhaps accidental, perhaps purposeful (rightly, Odets is ambiguous: to write otherwise would be vapid or schematic), provides a resolution as inevitable as that of a morality play, in which a sin against one's soul leads to other sins, then to death.

But Odets' theme rests on the faulty premise that music is an alternative to commerce. While the musician is an artist, he practises his art in a society governed by the same economy as boxing. Like a boxer who loses, a violinist who is not in an orchestra is out of work. And what pays for symphony orchestras? Chiefly, donations from wealthy businessmen.

Although *Rocket to the Moon* (1939) is essentially a

domestic drama about whether Ben Stark, a middle-aged dentist, will leave his wife Belle for his young receptionist Cleo, economics is a factor. His professional and marital frustrations mirror each other. Once a pioneer in orthodontia, he now earns little. His widowed partner earns less: he cannot afford to pay the office rent or care adequately for his child. Stark's nagging wife is as frustrated as he: having lost a child at birth she cannot bear other children. His wealthy father-in-law, Prince, urges Ben, 'Take a rocket to the moon!' and 'make a motto for yourself: "Out of the coffin by Labour Day!"' Middle-aged people unaccustomed to flight are unlikely to pilot a rocket and those with self-made coffins for self-protection are unlikely to burst out. Ben has a brief affair with Cleo but lacks the strength to leave his wife.

Two difficulties inhere in this drama. First, Odets' protagonist is a dentist. Although one understands rationally that a dentist tries to save teeth, one's chief emotional association is that he inflicts pain. Thus it is difficult to evoke much sympathy for his personal problems, however acute they may be. Second, Odets changes focus from Ben to Cleo, who spurns the types of love offered by three men: a one-night stand with a dance director for whom one girl is as good as another, an affair but not marriage with Ben, and marriage with old Prince, that is to say, debased art, weak love and decaying wealth. 'I'm looking for love', she exclaims, and adds, 'I don't ask for much.' Seeking 'a whole full world', she actually asks for a great deal. Since Odets does not depict her as more than an ordinary girl whose only attraction is youth, one finds it hard to comprehend Ben's and Prince's deep yearnings for her and to believe she might achieve her goals (Odets' evident intention). Despite the fine characterisations of Ben and Belle, this bifurcated play is dramatically deficient.

As in *Golden Boy*, efforts 'to make a living, to keep respect, to be in love' constitute 'war' in *Night Music* (1940). As in *Rocket*, the quest for love and a feeling of malaise are important. In *Night Music* a young man and woman find love in a world where rootlessness is more pervasive than in any other play by Odets. The characters are isolated personally, socially and perhaps metaphysically. Ultimately, Fay and Steve (whose nickname 'Suitcase Steve' indicates his homelessness) join to realise aspirations towards life and love that resemble those of Cleo. Love also dominates *Clash by Night* (1941), whose plot is the conventional triangle of husband–wife–lover. Here too society is a factor: the husband is not regularly employed and the lover worries if his job will last. But the play builds towards violence that includes murder.

Love, which becomes increasingly prominent in Odets' work, is present at the start and relates to society. As a character in *Rocket* says, in a virtual summary of Odets' view, love is not something apart from the totality of life, an entertainment for a spare hour. Because 'It's a synthesis of good and bad, economics, work, play, all contacts', it 'is no solution of life' but 'the opposite. You have to bring a whole balanced normal life to love if you want it to go.' Normality is absent in economically troubled times that make a woman not a wife but a dependent of a man unable to earn a living and ashamed to tell her so. Thus the marriage of Ben in *Rocket* sours, as does that of the son, also named Ben, in *Paradise Lost*. The love of Lorna and Joe Bonaparte ends in death. Elsewhere, characters without jobs defer marriage and children: Florence in *Lefty* and the daughter in *Paradise Lost*.

Perhaps Odets' most notable quality is language. His characters' speech combines American wisecracks, period slang, Jewish-American speech of the time and intrinsically apt imagery. *Golden Boy* abounds in wisecracks. Moody comments on a ringing telephone, 'If that's for me, tear it up. I ain't in, not even for God.' Answering it, Lorna tops him: 'It's Mrs. God – your wife'. Odets employs such 1930s slang as 'You know you're aces with me' (*Paradise Lost*). His Jewish-American idiom (to be discussed later) is accurate: 'Excuse me I ever lived' (*Paradise Lost*). Imagery springs from character. A cabby's wife: 'we're stalled like a flivver in the snow' (*Lefty*). A dentist: 'We're like two exposed nerves' (*Rocket*).

Too often, Odets lacks dialectic. Instead of arguing, with verbal thrust and parry, his characters tend to pontificate and sloganeer, especially near the final curtain. Such rhetoric is obvious in *Till the Day I Die*: 'Brothers will live in the soviets of the world. Yes, a world of security and freedom is waiting for all mankind!' Odets' upbeat finales are often generalised: 'Everywhere now men are rising from their sleep. Men, men are understanding! [. . .] No fruit tree wears a lock and key. Men will sing at their work, men will love. Ohhh, darling, the world is in its morning . . . and *no man fights alone*!' (*Paradise Lost*). In an interview with Arthur Wagner (*Harper's Magazine,* September 1966) Odets admits that his habit of 'tacking on a certain ideological posture' to his plays damaged them and that 'the material was always richer than the ideational direction that I tried to superimpose upon it'. Nevertheless, 'the life which was expressed, was impelled by some ideological direction in which I was going. It's almost like not trusting the material to make a statement, but you have to add a comment [. . .]. I should have learned a lesson from Ibsen; that it's simply enough to present the question.'

On the page, not the stage, one might overlook Odets' effective theatricality. A torture scene in *Till the Day I Die* has a Nazi make a violinist place his hands on a desk and slam a rifle butt on his fingers. One scene of *Rocket* ends with a passionate embrace. In his interview with Wagner Odets points to the origins of *Lefty* in the American minstrel show, which features an interlocutor, performers who do their specialties, and actors planted in the audience. Such plants were also used in agitprop plays to draw the real audience into the play's action. Odets' usage is exciting, notably in the labour spy episode, where an actor in the audience denounces the hireling who is his brother. Paradoxically, while theatricalism usually dispels illusion by reminding the audience it is watching a play, in *Lefty* it promotes the illusion that the audience is in a union meeting hall.

As an actor, then a writer, Odets developed in the Group Theatre, which was organised by Lee Strasberg, Cheryl Crawford and Harold Clurman, who tells its story in *The Fervent Years*. They sought to create unified productions in which, as Clurman says, 'the so-called interpretative elements of the theatre were really creative functions, so that plays were to be seen as artistic wholes, not as scripts adorned by acting and direction'. When in 1928 they broached their idea to actors, the oldest among them was Morris Carnovsky, aged 29. In 1931 they began under the auspices of the Theatre Guild, which gave them a play it had optioned, Paul Green's *House of Connelly*, a thousand dollars towards rehearsal expenses, and actors it had under contract. Typical of the Group's infectious idealism is that after Clurman had rejected a play by Maxwell Anderson, he asked for financial assistance, which Anderson instantly gave: fifteen hundred dollars. The Group's charter and subsequent actors constitute a roll of honour in the American theatre, including Carnovsky, Franchot Tone, Luther Adler, Stella Adler (his sister), Elia Kazan, Robert Lewis, John (then Jules) Garfield, Lee J. Cobb and Sanford

Meisner. In September it successfully presented Green's play under the Theatre Guild's auspices. In February 1932 it became independent.

Its rehearsal techniques – now orthodox, then unusual in America – derive from the Stanislavsky system (named after the co-founder of the Moscow Art Theatre). The Method, as it is often called in America, is just that, a means and not an end. In Clurman's words, the end 'is to enable the actor to use himself more consciously as an instrument for the attainment of truth on the stage'. The Method tries to permit him to depict with inner conviction and emotional reality the character in the situation. Because emotion is a result, Method rehearsals employ techniques to achieve it. One is to play what Stanislavsky calls a character's action, that is, his goal. In simple terms, a character might want to escape circumstances where others, obstacles to his goal, want to keep him. If he succeeds the emotion of joy results; if he fails, sadness. Another technique is improvisation: spontaneous, extemporaneous enactment of the basic situation of a scene in the actor's, not the dramatist's, words to free him from whatever might block truthful behaviour or feelings, which he would then employ with the dramatist's words. The Group also used – overused, they discovered – affective (emotion) memory. In this rehearsal technique the actor does not directly try to recall his experience of an emotion but to remember concrete, physical details of circumstances connected with it (furnishings, clothing, and so forth), thereby triggering a return of the emotion; still affected by it, he performs the scene.

In *The Country Girl* (1950), which deals with the theatre, Odets has a director employ some of these techniques, explained for the audience's benefit, to audition an actor, to whom he gives the character's action: 'Let's improvise the scene! Just the situation – not the author's scene! [. . .]

111

Ad-lib, just ad-lib it – improvise it. Look at me! I'm a fresh kid – I wanna marry your grandchild and you don't want me to.' During rehearsal the actor asks the meaning of a passage. The explanation takes the form of an action: 'Show that he's trying to win her over to his side.'

Group Theatre techniques inform Odets' plays, sometimes explicitly. *Till the Day I Die* calls for an improvised pinochle game '*in loud voices*'. In *Rocket* Prince repeatedly states his goal, finally with italicised emphasis: 'I try to take happiness by the throat! Remember, Dr. Benny, I want what I want. There are seven fundamental words in life, and one of these is love, and I don't have it! And another one is love, and I don't have it! *And the third of these is love, and I shall have it!*' Stage directions indicate actions: 'BELLE *begins to flirt with her husband*' and '*One attractive woman is an entire grandstand for* WAX. *Now he plays charmingly, eruditely for* CLEO.' Scenes call for affective memory: Edna recalls her daughter seeing an unaffordable grapefruit for the first time (*Lefty*), Steve recollects the early death of his mother (*Night Music*).

'Awake and Sing!'

Although *Awake and Sing!* was completed before *Lefty*, it opened a month later, 19 February 1935: time for the left-wing press to express disappointment at what it considered a step backward and the regular press to express satisfaction at Odets' broader thematic scope and greater technical skill. His first play, *Awake and Sing!* is his best. To most reviewers, it throbbed with vigour. Following *Lefty* it consolidated Odets' position as one of America's foremost dramatists. Walter Winchell, a political conservative, cried 'Bravodets!' Its characters were 'so alive' he felt he was their neighbour (*Daily Mirror*). Even those who hedged were laudatory: 'He may not be a master yet, but he has the ability to be one' (*New York Times*). Praising the Group Theatre's ensemble acting, reviews noted not only that this play, by one of its members, was well suited to its methods, but that the Group rose to the occasion and more than justified its existence. While reviews stressed the ensemble, they singled out individuals: Morris Carnovsky played the grandfather 'with endearing gentleness'(*New York Times*); as the mother Stella Adler avoided 'the worn out patterns of acting as the author has avoided them in writing' (*New York Evening Journal*); and John Garfield played the son 'with fiery force' (*New York Daily News*). Readers who have seen Garfield's films may, as they read Ralph's speeches, recall that force and the sincerity, warmth and almost naïve conviction he habitually brings to his roles.

Awake and Sing! centres on the Berger family, which the mother, Bessie, holds together during the Depression. Though working class with middle-class values, the Bergers represent a microcosm of society. Son Ralph is a blue-collar worker, daughter Hennie a white-collar worker. Grandfather Jacob is a skilled worker, a barber, and also a Marxist. For a time the ineffectual father Myron studied law, which links him to the professional classes. Brother Morty is a capitalist and Moe Axelrod, a boarder who lost a leg in the First World War, dabbles in rackets. The Depression informs the play: a nearby family evicted for non-payment of rent, Ralph's salary cut at the factory, a strike at Morty's plant, the inability to purchase anything more expensive than cinema tickets.

The basis of the action is melodrama: Bessie prevents Ralph from marrying a poor orphan girl; she forces Hennie, who is pregnant, to marry a naïve immigrant, Sam Feinschreiber; Jacob commits suicide so that Ralph, the beneficiary of his insurance policy, might escape the soul-destroying family. But how different the play is from melodrama! No one is a hero or a villain. Bessie acts not selfishly but to protect the family; the orphan, Blanche, is so emotionally weak that she gives up Ralph before he can act; when Hennie leaves her husband and child for Moe, an erstwhile lover, she receives Ralph's and apparently the author's approval. As in Chekhov's plays, emphasis is on character rather than incident; Odets disperses focus among several important characters; and dialogue shifts realistically from one subject to another in a single speech, such as Jacob's harangue against the imperialistic First World War, which ends: 'By money men the interests must be protected. Who gave you such a rotten haircut? Please (*fishing in his vest pocket*), give me for a cent a cigarette.' Odets knew little of Chekhov's work when he wrote the play, but he understood realistic dialogue and tailored his play to the Group Theatre. As he told Wagner, 'These early plays were made for the collective acting company technique. They're written for eight characters, with six or seven of the characters of equal importance. Well, this is purely from the Group Theatre ideal of a stage ensemble, and [. . .] this was how I wrote.'

Odets' characters reveal themselves. Morty responds to Moe's charge that as a businessman he is a racketeer: 'Don't make such remarks to me without proof. [. . .] I heard this remark before – a rich man's a crook who steals from the poor. [. . .] It's a big lie! [. . .] I started from a poor boy who worked on an ice wagon for two dollars a week. Pop's right here – he'll tell you. I made it honest. In the whole industry nobody's got a better name.' The Marxist Jacob confirms his son's statement: 'It's an exception, such success'. Later, Morty mentions that twice in the past week his striking workers 'threw stink bombs in the showroom. Wait! We'll give them strikes – in the kishkas [testicles] we'll give them' – a revelation that self-made businessmen deceive themselves about their honesty and that Jacob, who should know better, is imperceptive. Still later, Ralph discovers that half the pages of Jacob's radical books are uncut (he only partly understands what he preaches).

Odets' descriptions of his characters disclose their complexity, their thematic relationship, his affection for them, and statements or hints for Method actors. All the characters, says Odets, suggesting actions, *'struggle for life amidst petty conditions'*. Bessie *'is constantly arranging and taking care of her family'*, *'is afraid of utter poverty'*, and *'knows that when one lives in the jungle one must look out for the wild life'*. Ralph *'wants to know, wants to learn'*. Jacob *'is trying to find a right path for himself and the others'* but *'is a sentimentalist with no power to turn ideal to action'*. Even Schlosser, a janitor who infrequently appears, is relevant: because his wife ran away with another man, leaving him to raise their child, he is what Sam might become after Hennie leaves with Moe. The play provides opportunities for actors to use affective memory: Ralph recalls he cried in the lavatory during his birthdays, Moe his time in the trenches, Sam Hennie's taunts in bed.

Especially impressive is the play's language. One review quotes an unnamed dramatist: 'If this were put on in Ireland, its language would have for the Dubliners the same flavoursome, exotic quality that their speech has for us' (*Brooklyn Daily Eagle*). Odets is to Jewish New Yorkers of the 1930s what O'Casey is to Dubliners of the 1920s. Each artistically heightens his countrymen's real speech. *Awake and Sing!* opened the path for other Jewish-American writers to depict their experiences in the New World. 'How grateful I was to Odets!' reports Alfred Kazin. On the stage in *Awake and Sing!* 'with as much right as [. . .] Hamlet and Lear' were his 'mother and father and uncles and aunts', speaking a language that was 'always real but never flat, brilliantly authentic like no other theatre speech on Broadway', revealing a life that had been 'so long choked up', making him want 'to write with that cunning anger and flowing truth'.[2]

The language of this recently immigrant household reflects American clichés: 'You said a mouthful!' and, when a character drops a knife, 'You got dropsy tonight' and 'Company's coming'. Its Yiddish syntax relates to character. Bessie's 'Yinglish' often refers to food: 'You gave the dog eat?' The Marxist Jacob: 'So long labour lives it should increase private gain'. Sam, the most recent immigrant, speaks of Europe: 'To my father in the old country they did a joke'. The second-rate Myron uses second-hand language: clichés and paraphrases of what Teddy Roosevelt said (also a subtle indication that he lives in the past, since a different Roosevelt occupies the White House). The proud, self-made Morty continually calls himself 'a great boy' or 'a great one' for anything from 'smells' to 'the practical side'. The Americanised Hennie employs wisecracks (to his face she calls Moe 'a lousy fourflusher who'd steal the glasses off a blind man'), as does Moe ('All dolled up', he says to Ralph, 'What's it, the weekly visit to the cat house?') – typically American safety valves that hide emotion beneath a tough exterior. The most impressive use of language is Ralph's. At first he is inarticulate. What does he mean when he says, with apt American imagery, 'All I want's a chance to get to first base'? 'I mean something' and 'I don't know'. His description of Blanche achieves eloquence through an unaccustomed attempt at description: 'She's so beautiful you look at her and cry! She's like French words!' Remote and unattainable, her beauty makes him cry and she seems to have arrived from a different, exotic world. By the end of the play, as we will see, his language sings.

Another of Odets' achievements in this play is his portrayal of Jewish Americans, who had usually been sentimentalised as sage and spiritual, naïve and lovable, or vulgarised as comic greenhorns. The Jews of *Awake and Sing!* are newcomers or children of newcomers in a land whose materialism they deplore but accept to survive, who cling together as a family but are torn from it as cultural assimilation erodes its basis, whose struggle to get by clashes with non-materialist values that co-exist in uneasy, hypocritical tension or else collapse. Furthermore, the popular image of Jewish Americans is the family of *Awake and Sing!*: the domineering mother who strives to maintain family stability and simultaneously ensures that her children are grateful, the ineffectual husband, the Marxist grandfather, the wealthy relative, the youngest generation which has assimilated American culture yet retains ties with the oldest.[3]

One of Jacob's lessons is the need to abolish such families as the Bergers, which according to Marx and Engels' *Communist Manifesto*, where he read it, have reduced human relationships to monetary terms. As he says, 'Economics comes down like a ton of coal on the head'. Bessie prevents Ralph from marrying Blanche because the family needs his salary. Another reason for its destruction is the premium it places on middle-class respectability, which causes Bessie to entrap the naïve Sam in a loveless marriage with her pregnant daughter. Bessie's actions help to perpetuate this type of family.

While neither Ralph nor Hennie fully understands this lesson until the end of the play, they then help to enact it. Significantly, Jacob is at odds with his daughter (who represents this family) but is the confidant of his grandchildren: Hennie about her pregnancy, Ralph about Blanche. Odets shows Jacob helping the youngest generation. When Blanche telephones, Ralph quickly goes to the phone and Jacob '*pulls the curtains and stands there, a sentry on guard*'. Linguistically, Odets hints at an affinity between Ralph and Hennie. He complains of sitting 'with the blues', she 'Maybe I got the blues'. Moe, with whom she leaves, helps Ralph by telling him he is Jacob's beneficiary and by bluffing Bessie and Morty into admitting it to him: he theatens to give the insurance representative a note written by Jacob about the suicide, which would invalidate the policy (actually, the paper is blank). Jacob kills himself to enable Ralph, through his legacy, to leave the family and begin a decent life, but his suicide enables both grandchildren to accept two alternatives to the type of family he would abolish: flight or fight. Hennie chooses the former, Ralph the latter.

Odets foreshadows Hennie's decision. 'When I was your age it was already a big family with responsibilities', Bessie tells her before she learns she is pregnant. Hennie responds, '(*laughing*) Maybe that's what ails you, Mom'. Verbally linking her to himself, the one-legged Moe proposes she leaves her husband and child: 'The doctor said it – cut off your leg to save your life!' Surprisingly, some critics who approve Nora Helmer's flight from her husband and three children in *A Doll's House* object to Hennie's break with her family, perhaps because she leaves with a lover rather than *sola*. The alternative, however, is what Moe calls 'life in a coffin' and a continuation of the bourgeois family. Sam would become, if he is not already, a nonentity like Myron. 'I'm a lonely person', he says. 'Nobody likes me.' Myron consoles him: 'I like you, Sam'. Myron likes and is like him. With this husband and a child,

Hennie might become another Bessie if she were to remain, and neither she nor Sam would be happy. Her flight with Moe represents a chance of happiness for her and dramatises one way to reject such a family.

Ralph elects to fight. 'For years, I watched you grow up', Jacob tells him. 'Wait! You'll graduate from my university.' He urges Ralph not to become like himself, a man 'with good ideas, but only in the head. [. . .] This is why I tell you – DO! Do what is in your heart and you carry in yourself a revolution.' He pleads with Ralph not to marry, for marriage entails responsibilities that prevent action, but rather 'Go out and fight so life shouldn't be printed on dollar bills'. Since Blanche rejects him before he learns of Jacob's legacy, she frees him from any obligation to marry. When Bessie justifies her actions on the basis of familial responsibility he recognises that the economic system, not she personally, is at fault. He and his generation, he says, will do what she ironically suggests: 'go out and change the world if you don't like it'. Because Jacob's true legacy is not money but ideas, Ralph decides to let Bessie keep the insurance money: the life Jacob wanted for him is not, he quotes, 'printed on dollar bills'. Unlike Jacob, who did not read all his radical books, Ralph will, and he aims to act upon his ideas. Putting a book in his pocket, which is visually emphatic, he proposes to distribute ideas among items to be inventoried. 'Colletti to Driscoll to Berger – that's how we work. It's a team down the warehouse.' Despite racial or national differences, 'they're like me, looking for a chance to get to first base. Joe razzed me about my girl. But he don't know why. I'll tell him. Hell, he might tell me something I don't know. Get teams together all over.' Approvingly, Moe echoes Jacob: 'Graduation Day'. Unfortunately, films have made the American melting pot suggested by these names a cliché, but spoken by a young actor (Ralph has turned 22) with the sincerity, warmth and fervour of a John Garfield, the words would have conviction.

Ralph and Jacob quote the play's title, which is from *Isaiah*, 26:19: 'Awake and sing, ye that dwell in dust'. On that occasion, God will 'punish the inhabitants of the earth for their iniquity'. Odets' titular phrase is an exclamation, an injunction to do, not a description of what has been done. At the end of *Awake and Sing!* Ralph becomes lyrically articulate as he describes his resurrection: 'I saw that he was dead and I was born! I swear to God, I'm one week old! I want the whole city to hear it – fresh blood, arms. We got 'em. We're glad we're living.' The play ends with a visual image that reinforces his words: he *'stands full and strong in the doorway'*. Appropriately, Odets does not specify Ralph's course of action, much less his success. Despite the upbeat, recapitulatory nature of the end, Ralph joins no Communist Party. Happily, the 'certain ideological posture' Odets told Wagner he tacked on to his plays of this period is not ideologically specific in *Awake and Sing!* Ralph's song, as it were, is his self-awakening.

7
Thornton Wilder

If asked to select the most quintessentially American dramatist of the period 1918–45, O'Neill included, most theatregoers and readers would probably choose Thornton Wilder. Both in and outside the United States, his plays suggest archetypal America, which he celebrates as warm, innocent, religious, simple and simply nice. While they evoke small towns, Sunday schools and Independence Day picnics on the Fourth of July, the range of Wilder's knowledge is far from provincial. Leaving aside his novels, for which he is also famous, his plays draw directly upon such writers as Ben Jonson (*The Trumpet Shall Sound*, 1927), Johann Nestroy and Molière (*The Matchmaker*, 1938),[1] and James Joyce (*The Skin of Our Teeth*, 1942, from *Finnegans Wake* – by no means an easy read). Wilder's combination of literary sophistication and accessibility to mass audiences inconveniences critics more comfortable with pigeonholes. Although he is a yeasayer, his plays are neither simplistic nor naïve.

His theatrical forms are in the vanguard of modernism;

he was familiar with Pirandello's innovations and, after insubstantial apprentice drama published in the 1920s, developed a theatricalist, non-representational drama independently of, yet similar to, that of Bertolt Brecht. But his themes are not modernist: he does not urge social activism, convey despair at the human condition, or stress sexuality (except perhaps in Act II of *The Skin of Our Teeth*, though the heaviest breathing is the audience's laughter). Furthermore, he addresses not an élite but a wide public from philistines to intelligentsia. In what he recognises to be an American tradition, he writes as Walt Whitman does for 'a classless society' inclusive of 'everyone who could read or be read to'. Accepting Thoreau's admonition to simplify, he aims to reach that 'undifferentiated audience' which Melville sought when he wrote *Moby Dick*. 'The sublime does not wear a cothurnus' in America, a middle-class country that has no separate 'tradesman's entrance' for common language. All words enter the front door. 'In the very same sentence in which Melville apostrophizes divinity', Wilder notes as example, 'we are told that God had "bejuggled" many a man. It is a word from the skulduggeries of the country fair and the card game at the livery stable.' Unlike 'most European exercises in the sublime', he avoids 'high vagueness' to express noble sentiment and like Whitman embraces the common, humble and specific.[2] For a dramatist ('Some Thoughts on Playwriting') an awareness of so total a community imposes 'the necessity of treating material understandable by the larger number'. Wilder does not lower his standards but broadens his terms.

His homocentric drama reflects a wider tradition, that of humanism. The religious conviction that shapes it is non-doctrinal, non-sectarian, anti-puritanical and above all non-didactic. As he says with typical grace (Foreword to

The Angel That Troubled the Waters, 1928), he tries to express his religious views in a way 'that is a believer's concession to a contemporary standard of good manners'. To him, didacticism is a 'repellent' attempt to coerce 'another's free mind, even though one knows that in these matters beyond logic, beauty is the only persuasion'.

As a dramatist, Wilder's reputation rests on few plays: *Our Town* (1938), to be discussed later, *The Matchmaker*, *The Skin of Our Teeth* and three non-realistic one-act plays published in 1931: *The Long Christmas Dinner*, *The Happy Journey to Trenton and Camden* and *Pullman Car Hiawatha*.

At the end of the 1920s Wilder found theatre 'a minor art and an inconsequential diversion' (Preface to *Three Plays*). He blames 'the rise of the middle-classes – they wanted their theatre soothing'. He faults their 'aggressive complacency', a consequence of having to justify themselves while emerging from the shadow of the aristocracy. Sanctimoniously, they reassured themselves as to the worthiness of moneymaking, property and servants who knew their places. They ignored 'wide tracts of injustice' and 'shrank from contemplating those elements within themselves that were ridiculous, shallow, and harmful'. They 'fashioned a theatre which would not disturb them'. Although these statements should not prompt anyone to turn Thornton Wilder into Clifford Odets, they should alert one to a darker aspect of his art. The world he dramatises is multi-faceted.

Celebrating life, he contrasts it with death, which with suffering is prominent in almost all his plays (in the most notable exception, *The Matchmaker*, three major characters are widowed). *Pullman Car Hiawatha*, en route to Chicago, is for one character a journey to death. Another is insane and still another is the ghost of a worker killed while constructing a bridge over which the train passes. Revealed at the end, the reason for *The Happy Journey* is a family's visit to a daughter whose child died moments after birth. But death is present almost from the start, when the car stops to let a funeral pass. Though warm and affectionate, this picture of American family life has shadows. The mother's moralisms reduce her children to tears, after which she '*is suddenly joyously alive and happy*'. Spanning ninety years, as members of different generations arrive, partake of, and depart from *The Long Christmas Dinner*, Wilder celebrates the American family and the American experience. The oldest character recalls Indians, automobiles supplant horses, a factory springs up, someone joins the Alaska gold rush, European immigrants enter the community, the factory expands internationally, and young people leave the community as Americans become more mobile. Wilder laments the deterioration of the family and reveals sombre aspects of life. One character is an alcoholic, a vibrant girl becomes a sour spinster, a happy young father becomes a pompous businessman, a restless youth rebels against the dreariness of the small town, the factory's growth brings industrial pollution and urban decay that impinge upon the ritual celebration, and the play ends not with the promise of continuity but with the death of the last member of the family.

The Skin of Our Teeth deals with the survival of humanity by the slim margin of its title during three catastrophes: natural (the ice age), heavensent (the Flood), and manmade (war). Its originality lies largely in its treatment of serious and philosophical themes in terms of popular entertainment, which makes them accessible to mass audiences as well as the erudite. Reviews of the first production called it 'a cosmic variety show' (*New Republic*) and 'as easy to enjoy as a circus' (*New York Sun*). Wilder daringly juggles time, which as in medieval plays is one in the mind of God. Surviving the cataclysms, the Family Antrobus (*Anthropos*, Man) greets the ice age in its modest suburban home in New Jersey, the Biblical Flood on the broadwalk in Atlantic City (also New Jersey), and the end of a war in its home. Household pets in suburban America are a baby dinosaur and a baby mammoth, and those who flee the oncoming glacier include a Jewish judge named Moses, a Greek guitarist named Homer, and several sisters surnamed Muse, who are 'sort of music teachers . . . and one of them recites'. Antrobus invents the alphabet, the wheel, and brewing beer; before he has completed the first he telegraphs his wife via Indianlike smoke signals to save the family from freezing by burning everything except Shakespeare's books. Contemporary America mixes with prehistory as he becomes President of the Ancient and Honourable Order of Mammals, Subdivision Humans, at its annual convention where it receives from such other orders as Wings, Fins and Shells two representatives of each kind. Wilder does not portray the family as unquestionably good or the source of bliss. The unregenerate son who under his previous name, Cain, killed his brother is '*a representation of strong unreconciled evil*'. Significantly, since he is a product of his family, notably his father, he is renamed Henry, which derives from the German *Heimrih*, head of the family. Not only is no victor named in the war, but the survival of both Antrobus and Henry suggests stalemate and continuing conflict. One may read the play as either a celebration or a warning. Humanity may not survive the next catastrophe.

A hilarious farce, *The Matchmaker* contains such staples of the genre as people hiding beneath tables and behind screens, improbable coincidences, hairbreadth near-encounters, and men disguised as women. Set in Yonkers in

the 1880s, its title character begins by trying to arrange a
match between the miserly Vandergelder and the milliner
Irene Molloy; it ends with her own betrothal to him and
Irene's to one of Vandergelder's two overworked, under-
paid clerks, who take advantage of his trip to New York to
close shop and have what might be the only fling of their
lives in the big city. According to Wilder ('Noting the
Nature of Farce'), who points to the radicalism of
Beaumarchais' pre-1789 *Marriage of Figaro* as example,
farce provides 'social comment'. In *The Matchmaker*
Vandergelder advises the milliner: 'the aim of business is to
make profit. [. . .] You pay those girls of yours too much.
You pay them as much as men. Girls like that enjoy their
work. Wages, Mrs. Molloy, are paid to make people do
work they don't want to do.' Wilder also employs him to
describe women's position in society. He wishes to marry
because he likes a comfortable and economically run home.
'That's a woman's work; but even a woman can't do it well
if she's merely being paid for it. In order to run a house well,
a woman must have the feeling that she owns it. Marriage is
a bribe to make a housekeeper think she's a householder.'
And 'if women could harness their natures to something
higher than a house and a baby carriage – tck! tck! – they'd
change the world'. Although Wilder wrote the play during
the Depression, the underlying rebellion it urges, as this
speech demonstrates, is wider than worker against capitalist: it is the rebellion against all constraints that thwart a
rich, full life.

To Wilder, people should cherish life before it is too late.
As the Fortune Teller (*Skin of Our Teeth*) says, forecasting
the future is easy. 'But who can tell your past, eh? Nobody!
Your youth – where did it go? It slipped away while you
weren't looking.' Of one spectator she predicts, 'Next year
the watchsprings inside you will crumble up. Death by

regret, – Type Y. [. . .] You'll decide that you should have lived for pleasure, but that you missed it.' Even the most mundane aspects of existence, from wallpaper to parents to grammar school teachers, as the dying woman in *Pullman Car Hiawatha* recognises, foreshadowing *Our Town*, have immeasurable value. Few people treasure them as fully as they should while they can.

Dramatically and theatrically, he endows small events with universal significance. Dramatically, he relates detail to archetype, microcosm to macrocosm. Theatrically, he relates realistic to abstract.

In *The Long Christmas Dinner* time and activity are specific, but dramatic repetition during the play's ninety years turns them into ritual, endowing each dinner with significance beyond itself. *The Happy Journey* accurately reproduces American speech and behaviour, as when one child reads road signs: ' *"Fit-Rite Suspenders. The Working Man's Choice.*" Pa, why do they spell Rite that way?' 'So that it'll make you stop and ask about it, Missy.' The reading of two more signs stresses that everything children observe (sign, animal, person, activity) is new, a source of wonder. Adults link the small picture to the large. When the son asks how many people live in America, the father promptly replies, 'a hundred and twenty-six million' and the mother explicitly relates macrocosm to microcosm, 'And they all like to drive out in the evening with their children beside them'. In *Pullman Car Hiawatha* the date is exact, as are times of day, locations of berths in the car, and destination. Through narration and personification, Wilder sets details against a larger picture: geography (including Grover's Corners, Ohio), animal life (its population and the number of gophers, field mice, snakes and bugs in a nearby field), meteorology (weather information), recorded human thought (philosophers represent the hours), and the solar system – thus foreshadowing *Our Town* and *Skin of Our Teeth*. *The Matchmaker* utilises the conventions of farce to give the play's events ritualistic significance. Granted young people in search of a full life, of which love is a keystone, a grumpy skinflint who would thwart them, and a life-affirming matchmaker, one knows that whatever arises to frustrate the life-lovers, life and love will triumph to defeat or convert the miser.

Theatrically, Wilder juxtaposes the realistic and the abstract. Whereas the actor, a 'real' person, performs realistically, his scenic environment is frankly a stage. Wilder aims 'to capture not verisimilitude but reality'.[3] To this end, he turns to conventions like those of the non-realistic theatres of China (a character straddling a stick is on horseback), Japan (a Nōh actor's tour of the stage signifies a long journey), ancient Greece (the actor playing Medea is a woman), and Jacobean England (a bare stage represents different locales). Thus: 'I am not an innovator but a rediscoverer of forgotten goods and I hope a remover of obtrusive bric-a-brac.' According to Wilder, the realistic box set (three walls of a room) captures verisimilitude (what one individual experiences in one place at one time) but not reality (the 'generalized truth', abstracted to include all individuals everywhere). By removing realistic bric-à-brac, he tries to release persons and events from the particular to the abstract, thus universalising characters and incorporating fundamental experiences.

'No scenery is required' for *The Happy Journey*, reads a stage direction. A Stage Manager places and removes properties and reads roles of minor characters *'with little attempt at characterization, scarcely troubling himself to alter his voice even when he responds in the person of a child or woman'*; the automobile consists of four chairs, the rear two on a platform for visibility's sake. Although the

abstract setting universalises the experience, the realistic acting particularises it: the father holds an imaginary steering wheel and shifts imaginary gears, and all riders pantomime lurching forward and steadying themselves. In *The Long Christmas Dinner* the table and turkey look real; but actors mime eating and don wigs and shawls to convey aging; one side of the stage, where they enter, has a portal trimmed with flowers and fruit (birth) and the other, where they leave, is trimmed with black velvet (death). In *Pullman Car Hiawatha* the actors behave realistically, but the train is indicated by chairs within chalk marks on the stage floor; behind it is a runway from which two flights of stairs descend. As in *Our Town*, scenes begin and end by the announcement of the Stage Manager, who also calls for characters to appear, at times on the runway and stairs, to represent places through which the train travels, the hours (each a philospher who recites a statement) and planets (actors who make humming sounds). Wilder also portrays hours and planets this way in *Skin of Our Teeth*, whose theatricality smashes the fourth wall. To save the human race from extinction during the ice age, ushers in the audience pass chairs on to the stage to keep the fire going. To reach the ark that saves the Antrobuses from the Flood, they and pairs of each animal race up an aisle to the front of the theatre. The actress who plays Sabina hates this incomprehensible play and drops character to address the audience in what is supposedly her own person to lament the sorry state of the theatre and her fortunes that have reduced her to accept this rotten role. By avoiding veri-similitude, Wilder captures the universal. He does more. What one critic says of *The Skin of Our Teeth* applies to all these works: 'by eliminating clichés of [realistic] staging, he is able to offer the clichés of life as one kind of truth'.[4]

'Our Town'

Appropriately, because a major theme of *Our Town* is the transcendent value of the apparently banal, our analysis starts with two commonplace factors. First, the Stage Manager immediately names the play's author, director and chief actors: thereby indicating to the audience that the play is a fiction, not reality, and also thwarting our predisposition to regard the production in realistic terms. Second, he very early suggests that Grover's Corners, New Hampshire, to which the title refers, is not only the characters' town but ours as well. As a review reveals, the first production dramatised what the text hints: 'The house lights are still on when he first saunters across the stage and begins to put chairs in place. Now and then he looks out to see how the audience is coming, and takes a glance at his watch.' As he casually talks about Grover's Corners, 'The audience, taken directly into the narrator's confidence, becomes part of the town's population' (*New York Sun*). In Act III, set on a nearby hilltop, the Stage Manager, '*pointing down in the audience*', states, 'there, quite a ways down, is Grover's Corners'. At the play's end, the link is complete. 'Most everybody's asleep in Grover's Corners.' Then: 'Eleven o'clock in Grover's Corners. – You get a good rest, too. Good night.' On Broadway in 1938, when plays began at 8.30 p.m., *Our Town* rang down at about eleven. Grover's Corners time has become the audience's time, the play truly *our* town.

Grover's Corners is not real but prototypical: a fiction and part of 'our' American experience. Democratically and with artful simplicity, Wilder addresses *Our Town* to an undifferentiated audience of a classless society. The play's values are those of the ideal American small town in the stable, pre-internationalised period before the First World

War: democratic, egalitarian, middle-class, neighbourly and homespun. Wilder stresses Grover's Corner's community, not its potential divisiveness. While it has rich and poor, 'we try to take care of those that can't help themselves and those that can we leave alone'. In the first scene Doc Gibbs returns from the poorer section of town, where before dawn he helped deliver twins; he chats in democratic, neighbourly fashion with the newsboy and the man who delivers milk. Most of the townsfolk, minister included, tolerate the choirmaster's drunkenness. Repeatedly, characters call the town nice, unremarkable, ordinary and unimportant. If Grover's Corners were less ordinary it would be less archetypal. Its values are traditional, and as the state's name implies they are both American ('New') and also extend beyond the Union ('Hampshire'). The community is stable. 'Mortality and birth-rates are constant' and as late as 1913 it has no burglaries. Like life, Grover's Corners changes, though in small ways: 10 per cent of its high school graduates settle elsewhere; *almost* everyone marries; automobiles *begin* to replace horses. Essentially, however, 'things don't change much'.

The characters' experiences are typical. The older children of neighbouring families, George Gibbs and Emily Webb, attend school, marry and raise a family; she dies. Partly through the Gibbses and Webbs, but also independently of them – for the Stage Manager, literally managing the events on stage, introduces other characters to deliver different views of the town and sometimes plays their roles; begins and ends scenes to demonstrate characters or themes ('That'll do' concludes one); omnisciently explains ideas to the audience, albeit in a dry, folksy manner – Wilder focuses not on individuals but on 'our' archetypal town. Never sectarian or particularly theological (or for that matter grammatical), the play's religious views are homocentric and humanistic: 'everybody knows in their bones that *something* is eternal, and that something has to do with human beings'.

Our Town is ideal in the sense of archetype, not because it ignores unpleasantness. Emphasising kindliness and goodness, it does not hide the bleaker side of American small town life. Grover's Corners has a jail; while its citizens appreciate the beauties of nature, they are virtually uncultured (among the few books they read is Defoe's *Robinson Crusoe*, which celebrates the middle station of life); no fit place for an artist, the small town's stultification drives the choirmaster to drink and suicide. Mrs Webb's concern for her daughter points to its neglect of proper sex education: 'there's something downright cruel about sending our girls out into marriage this way. I hope some of her girl friends have told her a thing or two. It's cruel, I know, but I couldn't bring myself to say anything. I went into it blind as a bat myself. The whole world's wrong, that's what's the matter.' Nor does *Our Town* neglect darker aspects of life that go beyond a small town, including the waste of lives by war. Telling the audience what the future holds for characters other than the Gibbses and Webbs, the Stage Manager says of the newsboy Joe Crowell, Jr, 'Joe was a very bright fellow. He graduated with honours and got a scholarship to Boston Tech. – M.I.T., that is [Massachusetts Institute of Technology]. But the War broke out and Joe died in France. All that education for nothing.' Wilder, who a year earlier had rendered *A Doll's House* into English for Ruth Gordon, questions the institution of marriage. 'I've married two hundred couples in my day', the Stage Manager in the role of clergyman tells the audience. 'Do I believe in it? I don't know.'

The 1938 edition of *Our Town* and anthologies that

reprint it show more of a darker side than the 1957 version and the subsequent anthologies that conform to it.[5] For instance, the former contains more references to poverty and the increasing wealth of the banker. The more important deletions are a passage on the newsboy, one about religion, and one on George's possible future. When Joe Crowell, Jr's brother Si delivers papers in Act II, the Stage Manager reminds the audience, 'You remember about his brother? – all that education he's going to get and that'll be wasted'. In the original, the Stage Manager tells future generations, 'The religion at that time was Christianity. [. . .] Christianity strictly forbade killings, but you were allowed to kill human beings in war and government punishings.' In the soda fountain scene, during which George and Emily realise they love each other, George explains why he would attend college: 'I'm not only going to be just a farmer. After a while maybe I'll run for something to get elected. So your letters'll be very important to me; you know, telling me what's going on here and everything.' Her response: 'Just the same, three years is a long time'.

One consequence of these cuts is a softening of the play. The absence of additional reminders of the disagreeable somewhat reduces the play's dimensions. On the other hand, the play contains most of these subjects elsewhere, though often less forcefully; these deletions eliminate redundancy and avoid undue emphasis. When Joe's brother Si, for instance, delivers newspapers, the reference to Joe's death in the First World War (especially if the same actor plays both brothers) gives the audience a heightened awareness of the significance of Si's ordinary task, a major theme; yet since Wilder provides such awareness in connection with other characters, including Joe himself, the deletion here avoids repetition and makes the theme's later articulation more forceful. While the reference to religion and killing offers a view revealed nowhere else, the passage might have a prominence that would detract. The statement of George's ambition suggests that his decision to marry Emily rather than attend college is how Grover's Corners crushes youthful ambition and her response shows her manipulativeness; yet a non-political future makes George more typical and stresses tradition, not upward mobility; the deletion of her response makes her less manipulative, but this quality is still part of her character.

As Wilder says, *Our Town* aims 'to find a value above all price for the smallest events in our daily life' (Preface to *Three Plays*). Against the millenia of earthly existence, quotidian events might seem to lack significance; yet because life is fleeting each moment is precious and the apparently trivial details of an individual's life acquire value through one's awareness of them. *Our Town* celebrates the simplest, least pretentious type of life. If the most commonplace aspects of life have priceless value, consider the worth of what is not ordinary. When the Stage Manager says, before we see Doc Gibbs in 1901, that he will die in 1930 and have a hospital named for him, his mundane actions and chats become heightened in the spectator's eyes. At times, such as the introduction of the soda fountain scene, the Stage Manager establishes this perspective: 'I want you to try and remember what it was like when you were fifteen or sixteen. For some reason it is very hard to do: those days when even the little things in life could be almost too exciting to bear.'[6] Wilder also demonstrates unawareness. Because infants become children who become adolescents who become adults, one might expect parents – who often remark on the rapidity of these changes – to be aware of the value of small moments of life. Not so. Such exchanges as this, between daughter and mother, are all too frequent: 'I'm the brightest girl in school for my age. I have a wonderful memory.' 'Eat your breakfast.'

The fullest expression of this theme occurs in Act III, when the dead Emily receives an opportunity to visit the living, but with a painful condition: she is both participant and observer, living the moment and watching herself live it. She selects a relatively unimportant day. To Wilder, the most insignificant events of life are awesome. Returning to life on her twelfth birthday, she sees with wonder what will soon disappear: a pre-renovated drug store, a pre-automotive livery stable, a white fence 'that used to' surround her house, and her mother's youth ('I didn't know Mama was ever that young'). As onlooker, she sees, in the crucial sense of perceiving, that people do not pause to be happy or to express their love for each other. Life goes by too quickly. Soon, she can no longer bear to remain among the living and bids farewell to what, too late, she has come to appreciate: 'Good-by, world. Good-by, Grover's Corners . . . Mama and Popa. Good-by to clocks ticking . . . and Mama's sunflowers. And food and coffee. And new-ironed dresses and hot baths . . . and sleeping and waking up. Oh, earth, you're too wonderful for anybody to realize you.' As Wilder explains in his 1930 novel *The Woman of Andros*, in which a character returns to life under the same conditions as Emily: 'the living too are dead and [. . .] we can only be said to be alive in those moments when our hearts are conscious of our treasure'. Emily asks the Stage Manager, 'Do any human beings ever realize life while they live it? – every, every minute?' His answer: 'No. (*Pause*) The saints and poets, maybe – they do some.' Despite its poignance the scene is not a tearjerker. In his Preface to the Acting Edition Wilder advises the actress that the dominant emotion is one 'of wonder rather than of sadness'. Another factor that helps to prevent excessive sentimentality is non-didacticism. He does not admonish the audience to become like saints and poets. Furthermore, since the Stage Manager's 'No' applies to most people, what might inspire us might also depress us.

Our Town is a microcosm. Wilder ('A Preface to *Our Town*') presents 'the life of a village against the life of the stars'. With microscope and telescope, as it were, he dramatises ordinary life against a cosmic background. The play's three acts take place on four specific days, including the flashback, from 1899 (the year after a long economic depression) to 1913 (the year before the First World War). The Stage Manager offers a wealth of detail, including date, time of day, location of buildings and names on tombstones. He relates these to the universe: latitude and longitude, prehistoric fossils, 'sun and moon and stars'. As Wilder points out (Preface to *Three Plays*), 'The recurrent words in this play [. . .] are "hundreds", "thousands", and "millions" '. Husbands and wives eat thousands of meals together, for instance, millions of ancestors gather at a wedding. He juggles time. We observe the events of 7 May 1901, for example, but the Stage Manager addresses the audience in time that is its 'now' while a copy of the play is being placed in a cornerstone of a building for people a thousand years later and he refers to the automobile that will arrive five years from the play's 'now', life in Babylon thousands of years earlier, and rocks that are millions of years old.

The play's most celebrated juxtaposition of specific and universal is a letter addressed to 'Jane Crofut; The Crofut Farm; Grover's Corners; Sutton County; New Hampshire; United States of America. [. . .] Continent of North America; Western Hemisphere; the Earth; the Solar System; the Universe; the Mind of God.' Emblematic of the play's light tone is a teenage girl's comment on the address: 'And the postman brought it just the same'. Wilder goes further: he places *Our Town* in the larger context of western literary tradition. This letter, the finale of Act I, expands a passage in James Joyce's *Portrait of the Artist as a Young Man*. A reference in Act II combines the names of Mark Twain's most famous characters: 'Everybody always says that Tom Huckins drives [the hardware store wagon] like a crazy man'.[7] Act III repeats a portion, mentioned earlier, of Wilder's novel *The Woman of Andros*, which has Graeco-Roman sources.

The structure embodies a universal pattern: Act I, which early on reports birth, is titled 'The Daily Life'; the subjects of Act II are 'Love and Marriage'; Act III is about death, which illuminates life. Ritualistically, each act contains milkman, paperboy and breakfast. Binding the acts ritualistically is an appropriate song, 'Blessed be the tie that binds', rendered during choir practice in Act I, at the wedding in Act II, and during the funeral in Act III.

Because Wilder eliminates realistic scenery other than two trellises explicitly 'for those who think they have to have scenery', the theatrical form of *Our Town* reflects its thematic tension between real and abstract. The absence of scenery compels the spectator to focus on the details of life, not on the details of a setting. By contrast, the film version, which with Wilder's approval shows a realistic New England village, lacks the play's universality: the film seems to be 'about' one particular place, which does not emerge as archetypal.

Our Town is immensely theatrical. Actors planted in the audience ask questions about the town. Sound effects include a rooster crow, a factory whistle, and the town clock. The newsboy throws imaginary papers into imaginary doorways, children eat imaginary breakfasts, and George careens down Main Street throwing an imaginary baseball into the air and catching it (perhaps with an imaginary baseball glove). The tops of two ladders form upstairs rooms. In her white wedding gown Emily walks down a theatre aisle to the stage. The dead who appear in Act III sit quietly and patiently on three rows of ordinary chairs. Large, black umbrellas that virtually conceal mourners indicate a funeral; from behind this mass of black, Emily appears in a white dress to join the dead. The dead are calm, notes Wilder (Preface to the Acting Edition), and without 'fixed and unblinking' eyes. 'It is important to maintain a continual *dryness* of tone – the New England understatement of sentiment, of surprise, of tragedy. A shyness about emotion. [. . .] And in all the dealings of the mothers with their children where matter-of-factness overlays the concern.' The first production achieved this goal: 'the performance as a whole is subdued and understated. The scale is so large that the voices are never lifted' (*New York Times*).

Absence of scenery does not necessarily prevent illusion. Perhaps for this reason, Wilder in the same Preface notes two ways to produce the play:

One, with a constant subtle adjustment of lights and sound effects; and one through a still bolder acknowledgement of artifice and make-believe: the rooster's crow, the train and factory whistles and school bells frankly manmade and in the spirit of 'play'. I am inclined to think that this latter approach, though apparently 'amateurish' and rough at first, will prove the more stimulating in the end and will prepare for the large claim on attention and imagination in the last act. The scorn of verisimilitude throws all the greater emphasis on the ideas which the play hopes to offer.

The original production chose the second approach. The unseen clinking milk bottles became 'the spokesmen of time, symbols of the bigness of the little things' (*New York Post*). They would be especially effective today, when in America plastic-coated containers have all but replaced milk bottles.

'*No curtain. No scenery. The audience, arriving, sees an empty stage in half-light.*' So read the opening stage directions – misleadingly. As I learned when I directed the play, an empty stage does not always mean an undesigned stage. Mine had a dirty window and areas of corroded bricks that required whitewash and disguise to make the stage look empty in an aesthetically gratifying way that did not detract from the actors. The back wall of the Henry Miller Theatre, which housed the first production, was also disguised and designed: steam pipes lined it from side to side, almost from floor to top.

Unlike characterisation in the novel, says Wilder ('Some Thoughts on Playwriting'), which takes the form of the author's dogmatic assertion and his analysis of personages, that in the drama is formed by actors. 'Characterization in a play is like a blank check which the dramatist accords to the actor for him to fill in – not entirely blank, for a number of indications of individuality are already there, but to a far less definite and absolute degree than in the novel.' In the 1938 production the Stage Manager of Frank Craven (who in the film repeated the role, called a druggist) was 'homespun' (*New York Herald Tribune*), 'talking to the audience like an old pal chinning over the back fence' (*New York Post*). His 'serene, inexorable matter-of-factness [. . .] makes one quite definitely homesick, but pulls one up sharp if one begins to blubber about it' (*Partisan Review*). In a 1969 New York revival the role was played by an actor for whom many would agree 'it seems as if [it] had been written' (*Newsday*), Henry Fonda. This Nebraskan 'assumed an authentic New England accent, and from his first unobtrusive appearance' created the world of the play (*Wall Street Journal*) 'with quiet authority and grace' (*Villager*). As viewers of his films can appreciate, Fonda 'has a bent for the laconic that approaches genius', and he made 'the briefest and tritest phrase bear an extraordinary amount of weight' (*New Yorker*). In 1938 Martha Scott and John Craven, as Emily and George, emphasised 'simplicity [. . .] and the fresh wholesomeness of youth' (*New York World Telegram*). In the 1944 New York revival Montgomery Clift emphasised George's 'bashful' quality (*Morning Telegraph*). The role of Emily is more of a 'blank check' than one may imagine. An actress might play the soda fountain scene with shy innocence or as manipulating George to decide against going to college. Note, for example, Emily's repetitions and the statement that follows the pause, which suggests that she thinks before she speaks:

> GEORGE: Emily, if I go away to State Agricultural College next year, will you write me a letter once in a while?
> EMILY: I certainly will. I certainly will, George. . . .
> (*Pause*) It certainly seems like being away three years you'd get out of touch with things.

An objection to each interpretation is its extremity. Emily personifies neither pure naïvety nor utter unscrupulousness. One may incorporate aspects of warmth and innocence with early, tentative attempts to influence the boy she loves, a testing of her power.

Our Town is a rich, multi-faceted play; it is affectionate and aglow with humanity yet understated and not mawkish, intensely realistic in dramatic and theatrical detail yet abstract and universal, simple in tone yet complex in texture. While emphasising the positive aspects of archetypal America, it does not ignore negative aspects. Wilder's affirmation of humanistic values and American values is not a set of pious platitudes but the thoughtful conclusion of a humane and sophisticated dramatist. Its continuing popularity both in and outside America demonstrates the *our*ness of *Our Town*.

8
Lillian Hellman

Partly characterising Lillian Hellman's work are remarks in generally favourable reviews of the first production of her most frequently performed and anthologised play, *The Little Foxes* (1939). An 'odour of greasepaint and canvas pervades the drama', whose machinations recall those of Sardou (*New York Post*). It is 'a knowing job of construction' whose author 'writes with melodramatic abandon, plotting torture, death and thievery like the author of an old-time thriller. [. . .] In the end she tosses in a speech of social significance' that drenches the play with 'a Pinero frown of fustian morality' (*New York Times*). If these provided a complete picture there would be little justification for Hellman's inclusion in this book. They do not.

Aside from critical and popular success, two characteristics make her plays noteworthy. First, her melodramatic well-made plays (constructed according to mechanical formulae, with sensational, often hokey, effects) are parables, sometimes obvious, sometimes not. Symptomatic of triteness is the prominence of blackmail in all but one of her original plays (*Toys in the Attic*, 1960) and an adaptation (*Montserrat*, 1949). Second is her commercialisation of Ibsenite discussion, which Shaw in his groundbreaking *Quintessence of Ibsenism* called a technical innovation. In plays with villains, murders and the like, says Shaw, 'the idea of a discussion would clearly be ridiculous. There is nothing for sane people to discuss', and attempts to discuss 'the wickedness of such crimes is [. . .] in Milton's phrase [in *Comus*], "moral babble" '.[1] Hellman's themes of crime and her usually clearcut villains render discussion superfluous. As Shaw notes, Ibsen developed the art of 'trapping' the spectator, tricking him 'into forming a meanly false judgment, and then [convicting] him of it in the next act'; thus, 'we are not flattered spectators killing an idle hour with an ingenious and amusing entertainment: we are "guilty creatures sitting at a play" '.[2] Instead of entrapment and demonstration of our complicity, Hellman flatters us as superior to her villains and dupes. Unlike Ibsen's, her issues are cut-and-dried and her discussions confirm, not challenge, our judgments. What makes her plays fail as depictions of ethical issues makes them succeed as well-made melodramas. Furthermore, she is adept at characterisation and dialogue. Her skill in creating first-rate acting vehicles – particularly *The Children's Hour* (1934) and *The Little Foxes* – makes her well-made melodramas far more exciting on stage than on page, her discussions, babble or not, more riveting.

In *The Children's Hour* Mary Tilford, caught at a lie by Karen Wright, who with her friend Martha Dobie runs a girls' school she attends, is punished. Vengefully, she tells her wealthy grandmother another lie: Karen and Martha are lesbians. Mrs Tilford informs her friends, who withdraw their daughters from the school. Questioned by Joseph Cardin, Karen's fiancé, Mary's lie unravels, but she blackmails a schoolmate into supporting her. Wright and Dobie sue Mrs Tilford for slander and lose both case and livelihood. Mrs Tilford learns the truth and belatedly tries to make amends. But Karen has lost her fiancé and Martha, recognising she really loved Karen sexually, has committed suicide.

The Children's Hour has the paraphernalia of the well-made melodrama: revenge, suicide, blackmail, contrived coincidence (Karen conveniently arrives to overhear Mary's lie), secrets skilfully concealed and revealed (the means of blackmail, Martha's true feelings). Unlike well-made melodrama, however, punishments have no moral basis and no-one is rewarded: Karen loses her fiancé, Martha kills herself, and Mrs Tilford must live with the knowledge of what she has done.

Although homosexuality is a prominent subject, and the reason Boston, Chicago and London banned the play, it is not the chief theme. Nor is that theme malignant evil, which contemporary reviewers stressed. In the play's 1952 revival, when the House Un-American Activities Committee and its counterpart in the Senate popularly called the (Joseph) McCarthy Committee were destroying people's careers and lives, critics were closer to the mark in interpreting this work as an attack on the evil inflicted by slander. In *The Children's Hour* lives are destroyed by a big lie, which people more willingly believe than a small lie. Do these terms sound familiar? In 1933, while Hellman wrote the play, Hitler published *Mein Kampf*, which states: 'The great masses of people [. . .] will more easily fall victim to a big lie than to a small one'. During the period of composition, Hellman reports in the 'Julia' chapter of her autobiographical *Pentimento*, she was aware that Hitler would affect Americans' lives. Deliberately or not, *The Children's Hour* resonates the effect of people's belief in the big lie.

After the loss of the libel suit and the ruin of the Wright–Dobie school come three discussions of their ramifications. Only the first is well handled, since it logically derives from character and bears upon conduct. Although Cardin stood by Karen during the trial, she knew he secretly wondered whether Mary's lie might be true. She makes him admit this. Her response, 'No. Martha and I have never touched each other', satisfies him but shames him for his doubt. Aware that because of it she would never truly know if he believed her in future, she breaks their engagement. The second discussion, Martha's recognition of her homosexuality, is a shift of subject – a major weakness. Despite foreshadowing, its effect is claptrap, particularly since penance by suicide follows. After Mrs Tilford learns the truth comes the final, major discussion, which is 'moral babble'. She wants to apologise publicly and pay damages. Karen's initial rejection, on the ground that a rich woman wants to buy absolution, is nonsense, for Mrs Tilford asks to do what Karen demanded in her libel suit. Furthermore, 'it won't bring me peace, if that's what's worrying you'. After sentimental discussion of what needs no discussion, Karen agrees.

Days to Come (1936) also contains an untrue accusation: against a union leader for murdering a strikebreaker. A muddled play, it concerns management-labour relations that are initially good (despite losses, Rodman refused to cut his workers' wages for two years) but sour when he is forced to cut drastically in order to stay in business, worsen when the labourers strike, and crumble when he calls in strikebreakers whom he naïvely believes will not cause violence. When violence occurs the strike fails, the owner fires the strikebreakers, his marriage fails, and the good management-labour relations are irrevocably broken. Trappings of the well-made melodrama include murder, attempted frame-up, coincidence (Mrs Rodman is with the union leader when thugs dump a dead body outside union headquarters), attempted blackmail (of Mrs Rodman by the chief strikebreaker), secrets (the murderer, the unionist's alibi, Mrs Rodman's infidelity with her husband's partner) and numerous reversals. The play's major theme, the harm done by naïve people in their efforts to accomplish good, is simplistic and belaboured. In contrast to *The Children's Hour*, *Days to Come* has obvious contemporary meaning. Thus, the third act discussions contain nothing new: it is naïve to imagine one can break a strike without violence, frame-ups are standard in strikebreaking, workers' and employers' interests differ. Also, the discussion about the domestic difficulties that mirror the social problems trivialises them (at best adultery is a forced parallel, at worst irrelevant).

When *Watch on the Rhine* opened (April 1941) Hellman's parable was clear. The confrontation between pro- and anti-Nazis literally enters an American parlour as refugees force their hosts to take sides. Within the year before the play opened England evacuated over a third of a million British and French troops from Dunkirk, the Nazis bombed England, German soldiers entered Paris, Nazis continued to send Jews and non-Jews to concentration camps, and because of the Non-Aggression Pact between Germany and Russia American communists urged the United States to remain neutral and not to admit European refugees. In this melodramatic well-made play, Kurt Müller kills a Roumanian count who tries to blackmail him on threat of reporting him to the Nazi Embassy; coincidentally, they are house guests of Kurt's in-laws; a secret is gradually revealed (Kurt's importance to the Anti-Nazi crusade). As readers of *Pentimento* and viewers of the film *Julia* will recognise, his activity, delivering money to help

Hitler's enemies, is what Hellman did for her childhood friend Julia (a fictitious name, also that of Hellman's mother); and in *Pentimento* Hellman admits Kurt derives from Julia. Dramatically muddled, the issue becomes not whether Americans should oppose Hitler or be neutral but whether they should side with a decent family man or a smarmy childless collaborator. Discussion does not concern the merits or demerits of Nazism. After Kurt has killed the count, he tells his American hosts: 'I say, I will make Fanny and David understand. I say, how can I? Does one understand a killing? No. To hell with it, I say.' So says Hellman too. Instead of explanation she offers rhetoric and anecdotes about a melody, a staircase and an old dog. In 1941 such speeches were effective and the play, touching timely themes in a glossy, adroit manner, became a hit; but discussion is nominal.

When *The Searching Wind* opened (1944) its relevance was also obvious. With framing scenes in the present, Hellman suggests that America might have stopped the fascists before they become powerful. Chief figures are a diplomat, his wife and her rival. First flashback is Rome, October 1922, when Mussolini's troops took power from a willing King Victor Emmanuel. Next is Berlin, autumn 1923, during the Nazis' early anti-semitic riots which police and government permitted by non-interference. Third is Paris, September 1938, shortly before the Munich conference which came to symbolise appeasement since British Prime Minister Neville Chamberlain and French Premier Edouard Daladier agreed not to oppose Hitler's annexation of the Sudeten area of Czechoslovakia partly because they wanted to avoid war, partly because (blackmailing the democracies) Hitler promised to make no further territorial demands, and partly because he hinted he might in future rid Europe of the communist menace. Instead of proposing that America should influence England and France to oppose Germany, the diplomat sends a wishy-washy memorandum to Washington, condemning Hitler but urging tolerance of Chamberlain and Daladier for wanting to prevent their countries' sons from dying in war – as his wife does their son. Trivialising these scenes is a romantic triangle in which inaction or non-confrontation inadequately parallels the political theme. Melodramatically, the couple's son, wounded on the battlefield, must suffer from his parents' non-involvement: his leg will be amputated. Discussion in the final scene turns to Pinero-like fustian, for the audience agrees with the characters' conclusion: by action and non-appeasement, the democracies might have stopped the dictators from plunging the world into war and causing millions of casualties, and such mistakes should not be repeated.

'The Little Foxes'

The title of Hellman's most successful work derives from the *Song of Solomon*, 2:15: 'Take us the foxes, the little foxes, that spoil the vines, for out vines have tender grapes.' In performance, the play's contrivances enhance suspense and impact. It focuses on a rapacious southern family, Regina Giddens and her brothers Ben and Oscar Hubbard, who conclude a deal with a northern firm, Marshall and Company, to open a cotton mill in town. Their chief obstacle is Regina's husband Horace, who refuses to invest since the Hubbards would continue to exploit local workers. To make up the sum, Oscar's loutish son Leo, whom he wants to marry Regina's daughter Alexandra, steals Horace's bonds, kept in a safety-deposit box in his bank, intending to replace them before Horace learns they are gone. Discovering the theft, Horace decides to consider it a loan to deprive Regina of her share of the plunder. Because of his serious heart condition (at Regina's insistence, he returns prematurely from an out-of-state hospital), her fury and acrimony, including verbal emasculation, prompt a seizure. To save his life, she need only fetch medicine, which she refuses to do. As he crawls upstairs for it, she lets him die, then blackmails her brothers for a 75 per cent share in return for silence about the theft. But Alexandra deduces why her father was on the staircase when he died and determines to leave her mother and the town, as Horace, Oscar's badgered wife Birdie, and the black servant Addie had urged, to avoid entrapment by the ruthless Hubbards.

Melodramatics are prominent: theft, blackmail and murder. So are contrivances of the well-made play: secrets (Horace's refusal to invest, Leo's theft), coincidences (though Horace infrequently examines his safety-deposit box, he does so shortly after his return), and powerful act endings: Oscar hits his inebriated wife; Regina tells her ailing husband she hopes he dies soon; rejected by her daughter, she ascends the staircase alone. Yet Hellman avoids conventional rewards for virtue and punishments for vice. The virtuous Horace dies and Alexandra must for the first time face life on her own. Though rich, Ben and Oscar get much less than they want; without her daughter, Regina's victory is hollow.

The characters evenly divide into bad and good. Including the northern partner Marshall among the foxes, the villains number five. So do the virtuous: Horace, Alexandra, Birdie, and the black servants Addie and Cal. Their virtue consists chiefly of their opposition to the Hubbards, whose treatment of blacks they also deplore: Horace predicts the Hubbards' management of the mill will foment race hatred, and he ensures that Addie receives an inheritance by giving it to her in advance, in cash, rather than state his intentions in a will he knows the foxes will break; Addie charges that the Hubbards 'got mighty well-off cheating niggers', which Birdie confirms and also complains that unlike her parents, former southern aristo-crats, her husband prevents blacks from shooting game, which they need to avoid starvation. Music connects the virtuous whites: Alexandra plays piano duets with Birdie, who used to play duets with Horace, he on the violin. Yet the blacks are helpless because of their race, as Alexandra may be because of her youth and inexperience; Birdie is an alcoholic relic of a paternalistic slave-owning caste ('We were good to our people'); and the banker Horace is a repentant sinner whose practices once resembled those of the Hubbards ('I'll do no more harm now. I've done enough'). As none of her critics appears to have done, Hellman calls attention to one deficiency. Writing to Marc Blitzstein about the libretto of his 1949 operatic version, *Regina*, she observes that his 'whole approach to the Negro [. . .] is too sentimental. I think the original play had too much of such sentimentality and it was an artistic mistake.'[3]

Hellman differentiates the villains from each other. Marshall knows that the Hubbards will make profits by paying low wages to unorganised workers and is honest about his motives ('I want to make money'). Leo, who beats horses, is naïve and more slow-witted than his father Oscar, who beats his wife. Oscar is less intelligent than Ben – who spouts high-sounding motives, lets others act illegally (Leo's theft), and protects himself by refusing to hear details – and than Regina, whose verbal violence and physical inaction kill her husband. Ben and Regina, the cleverest schemers, bend Oscar to their wills, are composed during emergencies, and appreciate each other's manoeuvrings. Each is far-sighted: concluding much about Marshall's personal life from hints he dropped about his wife, Regina plans to use this information to enter Chicago society; Ben waits for the proper time to use his suspicion of how Horace died.

Hellman adroitly avoids the simplicities of good versus evil by emphasising the conflicts among the foxes, who try to manipulate each other. Ben tries to control the enterprise, Oscar to consolidate his fortune by marrying Leo to Alexandra, Regina to get more than her fair share. Hellman establishes a social foundation to the action. She sets the play in a small southern town in 1900, when the industrial revolution that had occurred in the north moved south as capitalists took advantage of states' investment initiatives and ununionised labour. Skilfully, Hellman also differentiates her characters through plans: whereas Regina would move to Chicago, a northern metropolis, Oscar sees no farther than a vacation spot on Jekyll Island, which is off Georgia, and Ben wants no vacation from moneymaking. Speech also differentiates them. Leo whines and wheedles. The irritable Oscar speaks '*nervously*' and with racist remarks. The composed Ben adopts the tone of sage head of the clan and tries to appear clever by using aphorisms, such as 'Modesty in the young is as excellent as it is rare'. Unlike Ben, who usually speaks softly and calmly, Regina, who dons feminine charm when it suits her, is brutally direct, though Ben has to interpret her meaning to Oscar. Whereas Ben's aphorisms are clichés, she turns her own witty phrases, as to Ben: 'Stay as you are. You will be rich and the rich don't have to be subtle.'

As usual, discussion takes the form of clearcut moral speeches that no one in the audience would question. Atypically, their ramifications are less clearcut. Addie states the theme: 'Well, there are people who eat the earth and eat all the people on it like in the Bible with the locusts. And other people who stand around and watch them do it. (*Softly*) Sometimes I think it ain't right to stand and watch them do it.' Though Hellman mutes Alexandra's moral fibre until the final scene, she carefully prepares it. In Act I Regina declares Alexandra old enough to go to Baltimore to retrieve Horace, then dictates that she should tell him to return for her sake. She is not meekly compliant: 'He may be too sick to travel. I couldn't make him think he had to come home for me, if he is too sick to.' Regina '*looks at her sharply, challengingly*': 'You *couldn't* do what I tell you to do, Alexandra?' 'No. I couldn't. If I thought it would hurt him.' Changing tactics, Regina persuades her that a return would be for Horace's good. When Birdie warns her that Regina and Oscar would force her to marry Leo, she '*firmly*' states, 'I'm grown now. Nobody can make me do anything.' Her later arrival with her father in Act II results from her initiative: 'Papa didn't feel well. The trip was too much for him, and I made him stop [overnight] and rest.' Thus, her self-assertion in Act III is plausible. Deducing how her father died, she refuses to go to Chicago with her mother: 'I'm going away from you. Because I want to. Because I know Papa would want me to.' Repeating Addie's observation, she determines not to stand by and watch people like the Hubbards devour the earth but to fight them. She earns Regina's admiration ('you have spirit, after all') and rejects her offer of friendship. The play's final line is hers, as Regina ascends the staircase alone: 'Are you afraid, Mama?'

Although the last scene is an uplifting testimony in behalf of virtue, unlike Ibsen's morally complex conclusions, what action Alexandra will take is unclear. 'I'll be fighting as hard as [Ben will] be fighting', she says, adding, 'someplace else'. A major change in the film version highlights the play's ambiguity. The film adds a character, a young journalist in love with Alexandra who opposes the Hubbards' exploitation of the townspeople. A fighting alternative to the foxes, he is also a rival to Leo, whom he socks on the jaw, knocking him down. At the film's end, he takes Alexandra away from her mother's home: a union of love and anti-Hubbard activism.

When *The Little Foxes* opened in February 1939, its thematic implications went beyond rapacity. Ben tells Regina, 'the world is open. Open for people like you and me. Ready for us, waiting for us. After all, this is just the beginning.' A parable, the play is as much about the potential despoilers of the *world* in 1939 as those of the American south in 1900. In 1937 Hellman had been in Spain under fascist bombardment during its civil war and as she left had begun to think about this play (*New York Times*, 26 February 1939). During her mission on behalf of Julia she narrowly escaped arrest by the Nazis in Berlin. In March 1938 Hitler annexed Austria; in May she learned the Nazis had killed Julia. While she wrote the play, America was bound by the isolationist Neutrality Act of 1937, which prevented intervention in Europe. It requires little imagination to recognise in the foxes the fascists who had begun to devour the earth, in the defeated Birdie decayed European aristocracy, in the dying banker Horace European capitalism too weak to intervene effectively, and in young Alexandra hope that America would fight.

At the heart of the original production's success was the Regina of Tallulah Bankhead, who 'using few of the old tricks' (*New York Mirror*) and 'sparing of the showy side' (*New York Times*) employed her 'husky, commanding voice' to cut 'clean through her staccato lines' (*New York World-Telegram*). Her 'crafty outwitting of her desperate brothers has the suavity of merciless laughter. Her performance, cloaked lightly in the buoyancy of her comic manner, suggests a combination of trademarked Southern charm and the spirit of the Borgias to breed a carbolic acid sugarfoot. She is Cindy Lou and Mme. Dracula, honeysuckle and deadly nightshade' (*New York Journal-American*). Dan Duryea (who repeated the role of Leo in the film) won praise for 'his idiot's whimperings and swagger', as did Frank Conroy (Horace) for 'the secure dignity with which he can walk or sit, or say yes or no without getting on a soapbox' (*New Republic*). In the film, Bette Davis omits, save for a moment in Regina's last encounter with her brothers, the mannerisms beloved by impersonators. Without triteness or overacting, she tells Horace with quiet determination that she hopes he will die soon; rather than spew venom when she says how contemptible she always found him, she recollects her emotion; and during his fatal heart attack she is stunned, then shocked at her luck, then (refusing to look at him) in almost painful suspense until he collapses.

In the 1967 New York revival Anne Bancroft played Regina with 'an icy composure' that helped 'to make her later eruptions more spectacularly emotional' (*Newark Evening News*). George C. Scott acted Ben as a 'grinning' and 'gravel-toned villain [. . .] exulting in villainy', without 'the cynical humour that [Charles] Dingle conveyed' in the 1939 production (and 1941 film); Margaret Leighton performed Birdie, 'her face ravaged with drink and agony, her voice thick with accepted despair' (*New York Times*), with 'a fragile quality' (*Variety*), in contrast to Patricia Collinge who (in the film and I infer first production) played a broken woman whose hopes the foxes repeatedly raise only to dash.

The most controversial Regina has been Elizabeth

Taylor in her stage debut (New York, 1981; London, 1982). Admirers say she 'has charm, grandeur and sex appeal' with 'the killer instinct [. . .] and the skill to project it from a stage' in 'a performance that begins gingerly, soon gathers steam and then explodes into a black and thunderous storm that may just knock you out of your seat' (*New York Times*); her portrayal is 'well thought out and skillfully modulated' and her final lines in Act II are 'like repeated blows in the face' at which 'the audience gasps [. . .] in mingled astonishment and pain' (*New Yorker*). To detractors her voice is 'squeaky and infantile', her movements 'lack grace and even maturity' (*New York*); with 'little technique' and 'little ability to take command' she has no 'power to sustain a long scene', and 'in the climaxes, her force comes from her throat, not her spirit; the result is only noise' (*Saturday Review*).

Of all Hellman's plays, *The Little Foxes* has been the most durable. Better crafted than her other works, it is varied in characterisation and language. Of particular importance to the theatre, it is an effective acting vehicle not only for a female star but also for supporting characters.

9
William Saroyan

In Saroyan the professional theatre finds a new type of American dramatist: born in, his mind formed by, California, where many of his plays are set. Writers considered so far, including Anderson, born in the midwest, and Hellman, born in the south, are identifiable with the upper eastern seaboard, often with literary and dramatic roots beyond the Atlantic Ocean. Even when they foray into California – Kaufman and Hart's *Once in a Lifetime*, for instance, or Odets' *The Big Knife* (1949) – the sensibilities that inform their plays remain on the east coast. Saroyan's temperament is that of the freewheeling Californian individualist, an American writ large. Road maps of the state of California proclaim it to be the 'Land of Superlatives', a word that fits the outlook and literary landscape of many California writers, including Saroyan. Marked by excess, his tales are tall, his personal and literary boundaries unrestricted.

To Saroyan grime hides purity, love is beautiful and universal, life can if you permit it be mellow or exuberant.

Although he began to write fiction and drama during the Depression, which they reflect, they also emphasise the love, friendship, neighbourliness and decency that surmount material deprivation. Neighbours bring food to the poor family of *My Heart's in the Highlands* (1939) so that a penniless old bugle player will continue to play; when the family is evicted, the father leaves his furniture for the new tenants partly because they too are poor, partly as a kind of barter for the rent he owes. Kindness and decency elevate Saroyan's people. In *Love's Old Sweet Song* (1940) a telegram delivery boy brings a collect wire, but because many people cannot afford to pay he memorises and recites the messages. Saroyan subscribes to the view of the father in *The Beautiful People* (1941): 'you cannot begin to change [the world] from the *outside*. The image of the good must first be real to the *mind* before it can inhabit substance and occupy space.' In *Sweeney in the Trees* (1940) the title character tosses fake money on the floor so that people may learn to despise money by kicking it. At the end of the play he throws real money, which they kick before realising it is genuine. They then divide it equally. One bill remains. They throw it out of the window: 'For somebody in the street'. Because, Saroyan believes, life requires more than bread, a fraud may become a saviour: in *Love's Old Sweet Song* a con-man sells a liquid that 'can do no harm, but it can cure nothing'. Therefore taking it 'is the taking of faith. And with these bottles I carry to the people what they need most. *Faith*. [. . .] I know of no other way in which to do anything about the wretchedness I see everywhere I go.'

Reviews of *The Time of Your Life* (1939) stress Saroyan's typical 'enthusiasm for all the living' (*New York Times*). To him, life is fun and 'the basic trouble with the American theatre is that the element of "play" has been completely forgotten' in favour of 'essays at one or another of the many variations of reality, usually sorrowful' (Preface to *Highlands*). Californianly, he is 'on the side of more instead of less', 'health instead of sickness, energy instead of dispiritedness, enjoyment instead of distaste' (Introduction to *The Time of Your Life and Other Plays*).

He insists 'that people are good, that living is good, that decency is right, that good is not only achievable but inevitable' (Preface to *Don't Go Away Mad*, 1943). A gambler, he puts his money on the ultimate victory of humanity, hence the title *Across the Board on Tomorrow Morning* (1941): to bet win, place and show on a horse symbolically named Tomorrow Morning. His characters choose goodness; for example, when a businessman who has sent pension cheques to the former occupant of the house in which Jonah's poor family lives learns that Jonah has cashed them despite the occupant's death years ago, he decides to send no more but later redecides to send them regularly, adding ten dollars (*The Beautiful People*).

Saroyan admires innocence and love. Among the dedicatees of *Highlands* are 'the pure in heart', 'the lowly and great, whose lives are poetry', 'the child grown old, and the child of childhood': in short, those whose hearts are in the highlands. In *Sweeney* he describes a 15-year-old boy as 'a genius' and a 73-year-old poet as '*a small boy*'. At times, innocence is immensely charming, as in *Highlands*, almost all of whose characters have it, notably a precocious boy who inspires affection partly because he understands both poverty and beauty, partly because Saroyan dramatises his charm (he cunningly persuades a grocer to provide food on credit). In *A Decent Birth, A Happy Funeral* (1941)[1] a stripper at the Gayety Theatre reads a fan letter from a nearly 90-year-old man who advises her to let her hair fall over her shoulders so that her audience will recognise her as the Biblical Esther. 'I am a Christian and once preached the Gospel, but now I am too old, and come to the Gayety to worship.' Unhappy about the war dead, he prays nightly 'for the mercy of God to reach the hearts of men'. He refuses to sign his name 'because I am an old man and do not want you for myself, as some old men do. I am glad you are so beautiful, though, because it is necessary for women to be beautiful if there is ever going to be any goodness in this evil and crazy old world.' 'Is he crazy?' she asks her fiancé, who replies, 'No man is crazy who lives to be almost ninety and then goes to the Gayety to worship'. At other times, innocence can be embarrassingly contrived, as in *The Beautiful People*, where a 17-year-old girl is called 'St. Agnes of the Mice' because she is good to them; according to her 15-year-old brother, 'the mice worship her' and when she is ill arrange flowers to spell her name. At the start of one scene, small flowers on the floor do just that. Preposterously, he goes to town to search inside a church organ for a missing mouse. When Saroyan later discloses that the boy, not the mice, arranged the flowers, his actions seem even more cloyingly sentimental. In *Love's Old Sweet Song* a large Oklahoma family passing through Bakersfield, California, leaves a little girl on the heroine's lawn, probably so that she and the con-man can (for the author's convenience) love the cute little tike, as she does them, and with the family's consent begin their marriage with a readymade child.

Innocence may join love to create exquisite beauty, notably in *Hello Out There* (1942), where a lonely boy in jail on a false charge of rape falls in love with an innocent, downtrodden girl whose plain appearance he eradicates by perceiving her inner beauty. Atypically for Saroyan, evil defeats innocence: though the woman's husband knows she lied about the rape, he kills the boy to save face among his friends, thereby leaving the girl more forlorn than before.

While many of Saroyan's love speeches have simple charm, many are pretentious, as in *Jim Dandy* (1941):[2] 'Where there is love, there is beauty. Where there is beauty, there is truth. Where there is truth, there is mercy. Where there is mercy, there is hope. Where there is hope, there is life everlasting and indestructible – new time, new weather, new sunshine, new rain, new grass, new flowers, new leaves, new blossoms, new fruit.'

Part of American lore is the notion that anyone can do or achieve anything; part of Californian lore, that he can be wonderful by his own criteria. 'Forty-seven years ago I made up my mind to be a great poet', says the old man in *Sweeney*. 'I am now – but only in the presence of people capable of greatness, and only by my own judgment – a drunkard.' The boy in *Highlands* is 'a genius' like himself, says his father, but more brilliant because he is young. Intrinsically, the individual has value and is a marvel of God's creation whose self-realisation is a joy. He is free to be himself. Characteristically, Saroyan claims 'Freedom' as the one quality of his writings that writing in general should have, and he calls the writer 'a spiritual anarchist, as in the depth of his soul every man is' (*Atlantic Monthly*, May 1955). Among the essential qualities of his work is 'spontaneity' (Preface to *Sweet Song*). He likes to give the impression that he dashes off his plays in bouts of inspiration, but he admits he makes numerous revisions.

He considers that anything a person does or experiences is worth attention. Thus, in his Preface to *The Time of Your Life* he records where he wrote the first draft, the typewriter he used, where he ate and what he smoked and drank. To be sure, one of his aims is comedy, and in *Love's Old Sweet Song* a salesman for *Time* magazine reels off in similar fashion the names of the entire editorial staff; but

Saroyan is also sincere. In *Jim Dandy* the title character speaks for him when he defines poetry as '*all* the experience of *all* the people' and animals too. 'It is *all* of the things on earth and *all* around it, seen or unseen, known or unknown', and all the past, present and future that was and was not, is and is not, will be and will not be. In short, 'Poetry is *all*. There is nothing which is not poetry.' Although such a statement is easy to deride by adapting W. S. Gilbert (*The Gondoliers*), that when everything is poetree then nothing is poetic, Saroyan's notion seems to be that with the proper spirit anything can become poetic, a term he appears to use as roughly synonymous with lyric and beautiful.

He eloquently defends a play against such critical charges as formlessness: 'Well, form is a big order and it means different things to different people. To me the play has flawless form. It starts right there with the first word, ends with the last, and in between goes everywhere without taking one step, and back again.' He dismisses the charge 'that it doesn't mean anything, or rather that it means perhaps too many things, none of them clearly defined. [. . .] It means what it means to whoever is watching, listening, or reading. What else could it possibly mean?' While it lacks conventional action, 'somehow or other a great deal happens, and none of it is strange, unfamiliar, unbelievable, or superdramatic. All of it is simultaneously delightful and annoying, laughable and heart-breaking, ridiculous and tragic.' He insists on its importance 'because it reveals what else can be done in the theatre, on the stage, and suggests to cleverer and more skillful playwrights a little of the enormity they have denied themselves through expert adjustment to reality and the market'.[3] The play is Samuel Beckett's *Waiting for Godot*. What is significant is

161

not simply Saroyan's appreciation but that he defends and praises *Godot* in the very terms he uses to defend and praise his own plays.

Oxymoronically perhaps, his sense of self-importance is engagingly unpretentious. He deflates himself without denying himself: 'I am great, and I am proud to be great. It is quite a responsibility. I might have been a car thief.'[4] Indeed, his plays include parody. He mocks Shakespeare: an old man, reciting Lear's speech on the heath, 'Blow, winds, and crack your cheeks', includes a few lines later Hamlet's 'To be or not to be' (*Highlands*). He parodies himself: 'And what do *you* want to be when you grow up?' 'Nothing. I'm a writer' (*Beautiful People*). He mocks his love of people: 'Please don't insult my friends. I hardly know them' (*Sweeney*). He sweetly spoofs political parties: 'You're a big important man.' 'No, George, I'm not big. And I'm not important. I'm a Republican' (*Sweet Song*).

Among the striking aspects of Saroyan's plays is their theatricality, much of which derives from vaudeville: short sketches, comic monologues, songs, dances and seemingly improvisatory comic dialogue. In *A Decent Birth, A Happy Funeral* a burlesque comedian dressed as a priest rolls a yo-yo and celebrates both the (apparent) death of a friend and the birth of another friend's child. *Across the Board*, about illusion and reality, creates comedy from stage illusion as various characters in the restaurant that is the play's setting discover that an audience is watching them. 'Who are those people?' asks a customer. 'New Yorkers, for the most part', says the waiter. 'A few out-of-towners.' Asked what they are doing, he replies, 'Watching us'. As a play reflects life, the breaking of one illusion breaks the other and the street outside the theatre, a character informs us, has vanished. In *Sweeney* a telephone rings, a man tells it to be quiet, a voice on the unlifted receiver speaks, the man disconnects it and throws it out of the window, another man (on whose head it lands) enters with it, it rings again, and he picks up the receiver to converse with the caller. *Jim Dandy* includes a character who enters swinging on a rope like Tarzan and a glass revolving door that, when turned, has bells tinkle and a globe of the earth above it light with blue water, brown islands and green continents. Songs and music figure prominently in most of Saroyan's plays – 'My Wonderful One', for instance, played on a piano to accompany an offstage cornet (*Beautiful People*) and bugle-playing (*Highlands*). Saroyan wrote songs for his plays (and with his cousin Ross Bagdasarian, who played the newsboy in *The Time of Your Life*, wrote 'Come On-a My House', which became a hit record by Rosemary Clooney).

'The Time of Your Life'

When *The Time of Your Life* opened on Broadway, reviewers recognised 'the sense of freedom which accompanies the laughter of the audience' (*Nation*) at a play that 'is poetic, far more so than some of the blank-verse efforts that help to give what is called poetic drama a black eye' (*New Republic*). With some phrases that would later attach to *The Skin of Our Teeth* and *Waiting for Godot*, the *Herald-Tribune* sums up the general view: 'A sort of cosmic vaudeville show, formless, plotless and shamelessly rambling, it is a helter-skelter mixture of humour, sentimentalism, philosophy and melodrama, and one of the most enchanting theatrical works imaginable.'

What suggests helter-skelter is partly a vaudeville mixture of stand-up comedy, dance and music with such theatrical activities as a gum-chewing contest that comically does not halt the dialogue of the chewers and partly a microcosm of America, present and past, including a high-society couple, a capitalist, a small businessman, *'an old Indian fighter'* who *'looks as if he might have been Kit Carson'*, a longshoreman, a newsboy, prostitutes and policemen, not to mention Americans of mixed races and national origins, such as black, Arab, Italian, Polish, Assyrian, Greek, Irish and Anglo-Irish. Yet all elements are connected musically by richly textured parallels and contrasts of incident, character and theme. In a seemingly irrelevant interlude, Joe tries to guess the name of a woman whose purse has the initials M. L. After an amiable chat she begins this exchange: 'Are you *really* in love with me?' 'Yes.' 'Is it the champagne?' 'Yes. Partly, at least.' 'If you don't see me again, will you be very unhappy?' 'Very.' 'I'm so pleased.' After bidding each other goodbye, she leaves and is never heard from or of again. But the scene is relevant, for it depicts adults who innocently fall in love without anticipating anything, including durability: paralleling the love of Tom and Kitty, which though sexual is innocent, and of Dudley and Elsie, which she believes cannot last.

Just as a line in *Waiting for Godot*, 'Nothing happens', is often used to describe its action (or inaction), the Arab's repeated statement about world affairs – 'No foundation. All the way down the line' – is often used to describe the structure (or non-structure) of *The Time of Your Life*. But events happen in *Godot* and *The Time of Your Life* has a solid foundation. Apart from its unity in terms of incidents, characters and themes, all more important to it than plot (which in many of Saroyan's plays is so loose as to defy summary), it is not plotless. Joe makes possible the marriage of the nice, dumb Tom, whose life he once saved and who serves as his general factotum, and Kitty, a pure-in-heart prostitute; and the personification of the American spirit, Kit Carson, kills the personification of evil, Blick, who blights the happiness of everyone at Nick's San Francisco saloon where most of the play is set. After Joe leaves to buy a book of poetry for Kitty to read while she waits for Tom, who has left to confirm a job arranged by Joe so that he may marry and support her, enabling her to quit her profession, enter Blick, head of the Vice Squad, in search of prostitutes to arrest. He is *'a heel'*, *'the sort of human being you dislike at sight'*, *'the strong man without strength – the weakling who uses force on the weaker'*. When he abuses Kitty verbally, Kit Carson defends her: 'You can't talk to a lady that way in *my* presence'. Blick takes him outside, beats him, and returns to debase Kitty, who falsely claims to have been in burlesque, by making her dance and strip. Joe returns but cannot kill Blick, whom Nick orders to leave. Waiting outside, Kit shoots him.

One reason the murder of Blick is not discordant is the appropriateness of evil killed by a symbol of America, and 1939 audiences, sensing that the world seemed 'about to go up in smoke' (Introduction to *Time*), saw in Blick the European fascists who threatened America (by implication, the good folk of the world may have to destroy international evildoers). Another is that the murder occurs offstage. Finally, Kit's report resembles his tall tales, which begin with the attention-catching question 'I don't suppose you ever fell in love with a midget weighting thirty-nine pounds?' and proceed with such unconnected and improbable (if not untrue) events as feeding lettuce, hay, salt, beer and aspirin to cattle; being fired upon seven times, presumably with a six-shooter, by a man with an iron claw in place of one hand; herding cattle in Toledo on a bicycle, ridden without hands in order to lasso the cows; and floating northeast atop a two-storey house swept along by a hurricane. His account of Blick: 'I shot a man once. In San Francisco. Shot him twice. In 1939, I think it was. In October [when the play opened]. Fellow named Blick or Glick or something like that. I couldn't stand the way he talked to ladies. Went up to my room and got my old pearl-handled revolver and waited for him on Pacific Street.' Blick's destruction is almost mythic.

In a prefatory Credo to the play, Saroyan writes:

> *In the time of your life, live — so that in that good time there shall be no ugliness or death for yourself or for any life your life touches. Seek goodness everywhere, and when it is found, bring it out of its hiding-place and let it be free and unashamed.* [. . .] *Discover in all things that which shines and is beyond corruption. Encourage virtue in whatever heart it may have been driven into secrecy and sorrow by the shame and terror of the world.* [. . .] *Have no shame in being kindly and gentle, but if the time comes in the time of your life to kill, kill and have no regret.*

In the post-atomic era, Saroyan repudiates the last view since 'if there can be a time to kill, then any time can be a time to kill' (Introduction to *Time*). Naïve or not (refusal to kill would not have prevented Hitler's triumph), the more recent belief is, the changed end of the film version demonstrates, destructive of the play's thematic integrity. In 1948 American films could not show the police unfavourably or let a police killer go unpunished. Accordingly, Blick became a police informer without legal connection to the law, and is not killed but merely thrown out of the bar: ineffective ways of depicting and combating evil (what is to prevent his return with accomplices?).

Epitomising Saroyan's 'paean to the essential goodness in life and people' (*Time*) is the story of young, ordinary

Willie's efforts to defeat a powerful world, exemplified by a pin-ball machine he plays throughout the play. 'You can't beat that machine', Nick warns him. Indicating Willie's parallel to Kit Carson, Saroyan explains that Willie's determination signifies the human against the machine and his *'skill and daring vs. the cunning and trickery of the novelty industry of America, and the whole challenging world'*. Willie *'is the last of the American pioneers, with nothing more to fight but the machine, with no other reward than lights going on and off, and six nickels for one. Before him is the last champion, the machine. He is the last challenger, the young man with nothing to do in the world.'* Just as Kit defeats institutionalised evil, so this young David defeats a Goliath-like industry. When he wins the game in the last act: *'The machine begins to make a special kind of noise. Lights go on and off. Some red, some green. A bell rings loudly six times.* [. . .] *An American flag jumps up.* WILLIE *comes to attention. Salutes.* [. . .] *A loud music-box version of the song "America."* ' Among the delightful aspects of his victory are that the machine itself seems jubilant, that the financial reward is insignificant, and that a little guy may have a moment of glory whose value is what he decides to give it.

The Time of Your Life keeps its sentimentality in perspective. Joe frequently puts coins in a juke box to hear 'The Missouri Waltz', which is *'played dreamily and softly, with perfect orchestral form, and with a theme of weeping in the horns repeated a number of times'*. But Tom wishes Joe would play other songs for a change and announces he is glad to run an errand since he will not have to hear it again. To Nick, Kitty is a two-dollar prostitute, to Joe 'one of the few truly innocent people I have ever known'. When she and Tom fall in love, comedy prevents mawkishness:

TOM: I love you.

KITTY: You want to go to my room? (TOM *can't answer*.) Have you got two dollars?

TOM: (*shaking his head with confusion*). I've got *five* dollars, but I *love* you.

KITTY: (*looking at him*). You want to spend *all* that money?

Humour balances the plight of the lovelorn Dudley, who speaks '*very eagerly*' into the telephone: 'Elsie, I'll jump in the bay if you don't marry me. Life isn't worth living without you. I can't sleep. I can't think of anything but you. All the time. Day and night and night and day. Elsie, I love you.' Then, after a pause: 'Is this Sunset 7-3-4-9? (*Pause*) 7943? [. . .] Well, what's *your* name? *Lorene*? Lorene Smith? [. . .] Where am I? At Nick's, on Pacific Street. [. . .] I'd like to meet *you*, too. [. . .] Sure. I'll wait for you.' Although Saroyan values intent and honesty in art, note the interplay of sincerity and irony in a longshoreman's appraisal of Harry's dance: 'It's awful, but it's honest and ambitious, like everything else in this great country. [. . .] Excellent. A most satisfying demonstration of the present state of the American body and soul. Son, you're a genius.'

If unrelieved sentimentality were all, *The Time of Your Life* would not reflect Depression America, world politics and capitalism, which it does. Wesley, an unemployed black, almost faints from hunger. Kitty's recollections of her past include her parents' loss of their farm (which 1939 audiences understood meant inability to meet mortgage payments). A strike and a battle with strikebreakers, assisted by the police, occurs offstage. Elsie agrees to sleep with Dudley in a cheap hotel room 'and dream that the world is beautiful, and that living is full of love and greatness' and try to 'forget debts' and 'the new pathetic war' on the horizon. 'Let's hurry, before they dress you, stand you in line, hand you a gun, and have you kill and be killed.' Perhaps because it cuts too closely to the bone, no one laughs at comically incongruous juxtapositions in Harry's stand-up routine, which includes references to poverty and war. Joe spends his waking hours drinking champagne to try to live 'a life that can't hurt any other life'. He explains how he can afford to do so: 'If anybody's got any money – to hoard or to throw away – you can be sure he stole it from other people. Not from rich people who can spare it, but from poor people who can't. From their lives and from their dreams. I'm no exception. [. . .] Loafing around this way, I *still* hurt people. The money itself earns *more*. [. . .] Money is the guiltiest thing in the world. It stinks.' Saroyan does not preach social activism but spiritual regeneration and efforts to help not hurt people.

Just as *The Time of Your Life* mixes sentimentality with comedy, irony and social resonances, so it employs some stereotypes (Tom is a sweet dope, Blick a villain) and subverts others. A prostitute who is innocent inside, Kitty also requires adjustment to life without a plurality of men, and her pleasant dreams of her family are, as she recognises, nostalgia for what she has known only in dreams. Like Kitty a subverted stereotype, the similarly named Kit, a teller of tall tales, derives from the braggart, cowardly warrior; but Kit is not cowardly.

In the 1939 production, Eddie Dowling played Joe 'with delightful unction' (*Nation*), 'warmth, affection and a gentle, easy inquisitiveness' (*Brooklyn Daily Eagle*); his performance was 'subtly understated and perceptive, apparently casual and yet rich with character' (*New York Sun*). In the 1955 revival, Franchot Tone played him with 'the detachment and the introspection of [a] saloon mystic' (*Women's Wear Daily*) and 'a bemused and quiet irony, interrupted by flashes of an almost boyish hysteria' (*Herald Tribune*). Some reviews compared them: 'Tone's Joe is older; his enthusiasm for life and people is as understanding but more offhand' (*Catholic World*); 'Franchot Tone seems specifically drunk, where Eddie Dowling [. . .] had only an indefinable moonstruck quality [. . .]. The difference might be described as that between an extremely intelligent actor playing a boozy mystic and a wonderfully bemused and spiritually cockeyed Irishman playing himself' (*New Yorker*). As Kitty in 1939, Julie Haydon was cast against type (the previous season she was the saintly Brigid in Paul Vincent Carroll's *Shadow and Substance*). Here was no greasepaint prostitute with a voice 'whisky-soaked enough to sound like an asthmatic foghorn' but a person 'of almost phosphorescent innocence' (*New York Post*) with 'fragile, incandescent beauty' (*Women's Wear Daily*). In the 1955 revival, Lenka Peterson was a 'rueful and distraught' Kitty who 'detests the life she is leading' (*Women's Wear Daily*). Unknown in 1939, Gene Kelly drew praise as 'a dancer of remarkable grace and versatility' (*New York Post*); in 1940 he was succeeded by his younger brother Fred, who 'duplicated Gene's success' (*Morning Telegraph*).

Saroyan calls *Love's Old Sweet Song* 'naïve and sophisticated' (Preface), but inaccurately, since it lacks the latter quality. However, the phrase fits *The Time of Your Life*. At his best, as in this play, Saroyan has decent people confront a malignant force, which offsets their values; at his worst, the goodness he cherishes washes out in banal sentimentality and strained lyricism. At his best, his drama evokes with engaging theatricality innocence, love, warmth and the sheer delight of living; at his worst, it is cloying and self-indulgent. His assets and liabilities are parts of the same coin which in his best plays shows a shining *recto* side and hides the *verso*.

10
Looking Back

Having removed these American dramatists from O'Neill's shadow, the intrinsic value of their work seems more remarkable than it otherwise might. In their time, Americans usually recognised these writers' merit, as did Europeans. Among the characteristics of modern drama is the withering away of national boundaries. A new play in one country pops up in another in a year or two, sometimes sooner: in 1921 Pirandello's *Six Characters in Search of an Author* opened in Rome and Milan, in 1922 in London and New York, in 1923 in Paris; in 1923 Shaw's *Saint Joan* opened in New York, in 1924 in London. After the First World War, when American drama came of age, dramatic traffic across the Atlantic went in both directions. In the late 1920s, Firmin Gémier, then director of the Odéon Theatre in Paris, told the American critic Joseph Wood Krutch that Moscow and New York were 'the only two cities in the world where the stage is really interesting today'.[1] As the German critic Julius Bab observed in 1931, however, the Soviet stage was interesting because of its innovative stagecraft but its new plays were 'only a naïve imitation of very old European forms'. The new American drama appeared 'much more promising' and though he regarded O'Neill as America's foremost playwright, Europeans were familiar with the 'notable' plays of others, including Rice and Anderson.[2] For the first time European theatres were producing many American plays.

At first, the major similarity of the dramatists discussed in this book may seem to be their dissimilarity from each other, their embodiment of individualism associated with America. In fact, their plays contain individualists (especially the Vanderhof-Sycamore family in *You Can't Take It With You*). Paradoxically, they also reflect Americans reduced to cipherdom (*The Adding Machine*) and Americans united by a common heritage (*Our Town*). Individualism suggests rebellion, which thematically (Anderson, Odets) or formally (Cummings, Saroyan) unites all these writers, including Wilder. To a greater or lesser degree in individual works, they employ comedy, including Anderson in his verse tragedies.

Many of their plays have social specificity: New York melting-pot (*Street Scene*), small-town south (*Little Foxes*). Recent events inform many: the Sacco–Vanzetti case, two plays by Anderson; though Odets claims *Waiting for Lefty* is a work of creative imagination (it is) as he was not a union member (true), its framework derives from an actual incident: a taxi union strike meeting was delayed when a leader did not appear (he was drugged, not killed as in the play).[3] But specificity occurs where one might least expect it: *The Adding Machine* alludes to then-widespread lynchings and burnings of blacks in the south; in *The Time of Your Life* Joe takes Kitty and Tom to dine and dance in a restaurant at the poetically named Half Moon Bay, a real

172

town south of San Francisco, named after the shape of the sand by the Pacific Ocean.

Unsurprisingly, these plays have roots in American life – *Our Town* reflects small-town America, *Awake and Sing!* the Jewish-American experience – and in popular American culture: *Him*, *Once in a Lifetime*. Also unsurprisingly, those written during the Depression – including *You Can't Take It With You* and *The Time of Your Life* – reflect it. Less surprisingly, they reflect recent events in Europe (even *Him* satirises Italian fascists).

At their best, these works have distinctively American vitality and affirmation, as if this first wave of important American dramatists were proclaiming to the Old World the buoyant energies of the New and its faith in the future, however precarious the present seemed. Yet let us try to maintain a sense of proportion. Even the best American drama of 1918–45 infrequently attains the stature of great international drama. But this statement also holds for the drama of any country of this or any period. Different ages regard plays differently, for people view them from changed perspectives (unlike us and like his contemporaries, for example, Samuel Johnson preferred Nahum Tate's drastically altered *King Lear* to Shakespeare's original). Many, myself included, consider *Our Town* a classic, but will many do so in the next century? A few, including myself and the reviewer quoted at the end of the Cummings chapter, hope that someday *Him* will become standard in American Literature syllabi and a repertory staple, but will it? Today, many plays discussed in this book seem strikingly theatrical. Whatever their limitations, they have considerable assets. Despite possible gaucheries, would anyone seriously claim that *The Adding Machine* is less theatrically viable than an expressionistic play by a

German or by O'Neill? The better American plays of this period – *Awake and Sing!* not *Till the Day I Die*, *The Time of Your Life* not *The Beautiful People* – speak to us today from both page and stage. To name only two cities and one year, New York and London revivals in 1983 include *You Can't Take It With You*, *Him*, *Waiting for Lefty* and *The Time of Your Life*. *Our Town* is frequently staged, as are *The Adding Machine* and *The Little Foxes*. Looking back at the plays of this period, one is struck by much that remains fresh. At its best, the American drama of 1918–45, including and excluding O'Neill, still has vigour.

References

1. Watershed Years

1. George Jean Nathan, *Mr. George Jean Nathan Presents* (New York: Knopf, 1917), p. 293.
2. Clayton Hamilton, *The Theory of the Theatre* (New York: Henry Holt, 1910), pp. 233–4.
3. Clayton Hamilton, *Conversations on Contemporary Drama* (New York: Macmillan, 1925), pp. 187, 196.
4. Horst Frenz, *Eugene O'Neill* (New York: Ungar, 1971), p. 5.
5. Elmer Rice, *Minority Report* (New York: Simon and Schuster, 1963), p. 178. Unless otherwise indicated, quotations and paraphrases of Rice are from this book.

2. Elmer Rice

1. Thomas Allen Greenfield, *Work and the Work Ethic in*

American Drama 1920—1970 (Columbia: University of Missouri Press, 1982), p. 51.

2. Mardi Valgemae, *Accelerated Grimace* (Carbondale: Southern Illinois University Press, 1972), p. 66.

3. William R. Elwood, 'An Interview with Elmer Rice on Expressionism', *Educational Theatre Journal*, 20 (March 1968), 6.

4. Wassily Kandinsky, 'The Problem of Form', in *Voices of German Expressionism*, Victor H. Miesel (ed.) (Englewood Cliffs: Prentice-Hall, 1970), p. 53.

5. In 1947 *Street Scene* opened as an opera, book by Rice, music by Kurt Weill and libretto by Langston Hughes.

6. Robert Hogan, *The Independence of Elmer Rice* (Carbondale: Southern Illinois University Press, 1965), pp. 131–2.

7. Elmer Rice, *The Living Theatre* (New York: Harper and Brothers, 1959), pp. 163–4.

3. E. E. Cummings

1. Eric Bentley, *From the Modern Repertoire*, Series Two (Bloomington: Indiana University Press, 1952), pp. 485–6.

2. For many ideas, the section on *Him* is indebted to Daniel C. Gerould. See our 'A Mirror Surrounded by Mirrors: E. E. Cummings' *Him*', which first appeared in *Players*, 44 (December 1968–January 1969), 54–6, then in our *Avant-Garde Drama* (New York: Bantam, 1969; rpt. New York: Crowell, 1976).

3. These quotations and paraphrases are from Cummings' essays in *Vanity Fair* from 1925 to 1927, collected in E. E. Cummings, *A Miscellany* (New York: Argophile Press, 1958).

4. Richard S. Kennedy, *Dreams in the Mirror* (New York: Liveright, 1980), p. 504.

5. Norman Friedman, *E. E. Cummings* (Carbondale: Southern Illinois University Press, 1964), p. 58.

References

4. George S. Kaufman and Moss Hart

1. Malcolm Goldstein, *George S. Kaufman* (New York: Oxford University Press, 1979), p. 299.
2. Howard Teichmann, *George S. Kaufman* (New York: Atheneum, 1972), p. 142.

5. Maxwell Anderson

1. Maxwell Anderson, *Off Broadway* (New York: William Sloane, 1947), pp. 27–8. Hereafter, page references to this collection of essays will be made parenthetically in the text.
2. Letters, 15 January 1874 and 25 May 1883, in *Dramatic Theory and Criticism*, Dukore (ed.) (New York: Holt, Rinehart & Winston, 1974), pp. 560–1.
3. Alan R. Thompson, *The Anatomy of Drama* (Berkeley: University of California Press, 1946), pp. 385–6.
4. George Jean Nathan, *The Morning After the First Night* (New York: Knopf, 1938), pp. 43–4.
5. T. S. Eliot, *On Poetry and Poets* (New York: Noonday Press, 1973), p. 89.
6. Laurence G. Avery (ed.), *Dramatist in America* (Chapel Hill: University of North Carolina Press, 1977), p. 313.
7. John B. Jones, 'Shakespeare as Myth and the Structure of *Winterset*', *Educational Theatre Journal*, 25 (March 1973), 44.
8. Eleanor Flexner, *American Playwrights: 1918—1938* (New York: Simon and Schuster, n.d.), p. 112.
9. Ibid., p. 113.

6. Clifford Odets

1. In his introduction to the 1939 Modern Library edition of

Six Plays, Odets disingenuously says he has not rewritten them. Actually, he cut a scene from *Lefty* (but forgot to change the number of strike committeemen) in which a young actor learns that because a play is a business investment producers take no chances on newcomers, however talented they may be, and cast to type. A receptionist proposes he read *The Communist Manifesto* and become militant. The only pro-communist scene in the play, it is trite and too explicit. Its omission gives the episodes symmetry: a regular alternation of scenes with cabbies of working-class origin and those formerly of the professional classes.

2. Alfred Kazin, *Starting Out in the Thirties* (Boston: Little, Brown, 1965), pp. 80–2.

3. I am indebted for much of this paragraph to Robert Warshow, *The Immediate Experience* (New York: Atheneum, 1971), pp. 55–67.

7. Thornton Wilder

1. With only minor revisions in 1954, it is essentially *The Merchant of Yonkers* (1938) retitled. Perhaps better known in its musical manifestation, *Hello, Dolly* (1964), *The Matchmaker* derives from Johann Nestroy's nineteenth-century comedy *Einen Jux will er sich Machen*, itself a version of John Oxenford's English comedy *A Day Well Spent*, and from Molière's *The Miser*. In 1981 Tom Stoppard adapted Nestroy's play as *On the Razzle*.

2. Thornton Wilder, 'American Characteristics', in *American Characteristics and Other Essays*, Donald Gallup (ed.) (New York: Harper and Row, 1979), pp. 30–2. Unless otherwise indicated, quotations of Wilder's essays, cited by title, are from this collection.

3. Quotations and paraphrases in this paragraph are from Wilder's Preface to *Three Plays* and 'Some Thoughts on Playwriting'.

4. Donald Haberman, *The Plays of Thornton Wilder* (Middletown, Conn.: Wesleyan University Press, 1969), p. 72.

5. These are *Our Town* (New York: Coward-McCann, 1938) and *Three Plays* (New York: Harper and Row, 1957). An Acting

Edition published in 1939 by Coward-McCann in co-operation with Samuel French of New York has transpositions, alterations and deletions of mostly the same passages as those in the 1957 text. Because all the deletions I cite are the same in the 1939 and 1957 texts, I do not treat the Acting Edition as a separate version.

6. The 1957 text cuts the ages and the explanation of this difficulty.

7. Winfield Townley Scott, *Exiles and Fabrications* (Garden City, N.Y.: Doubleday, 1961), p. 84*n*.

8. Lillian Hellman

1. George Bernard Shaw, in *Dramatic Theory and Criticism*, Dukore (ed.) (New York: Holt, Rinehart & Winston, 1974), pp. 638–9.

2. Ibid., pp. 646–7.

3. Richard Moody, *Lillian Hellman: Playwright* (New York: Pegasus, 1972), p. 201.

9. William Saroyan

1. So Saroyan recollects in his Preface, published 1951, but references to the Second World War, which America entered after the Japanese bombed Pearl Harbor on 7 December 1941, suggest 1942 at earliest.

2. The year of composition and first performance. Saroyan did not publish it until 1947 in what must be a revised version, for it has references to atomic power.

3. William Saroyan, *I Used To Believe I Had Forever Now I'm Not So Sure* (New York: Cowles, 1968), p. 102.

4. William Saroyan, *Here Comes There Goes You Know Who* (New York: Simon and Schuster, 1961), p. 228.

179

10. Looking Back

1. Joseph Wood Krutch, *'Modernism' in Modern Drama* (Ithaca: Cornell University Press, 1960), p. 104.

2. Oscar Cargill *et al.*, *O'Neill and His Plays* (New York: New York University Press, 1963), pp. 347–8.

3. Margaret Brenman-Gibson, *Clifford Odets: American Playwright* (New York: Atheneum, 1981), pp. 283–4.

Selected Bibliography

Unlike some dramatists, most of those discussed in this book either do not have standard editions of their plays or such editions are out of print. However, most of their chief plays, certainly those selected for more intensive study, are available in different editions of single texts, collections of plays by individual authors, and anthologies of modern verse or modern American drama.

Considerations of space demand a selected bibliography of secondary sources. Those listed below, which I have found useful, do not in all cases duplicate citations in footnotes. After the category *General*, which cites works that deal with more than one dramatist discussed in this book, are categories on specific playwrights. One collection of plays, by Saroyan, appears below because it contains important prefatory essays to individual plays and to the collection.

GENERAL

Bigsby, C. W. E., *A Critical Introduction to Twentieth-Century American Drama*, Vol. I: 1900–1940 (Cambridge: Cambridge University Press, 1982)

Downer, Alan, *Fifty Years of American Drama: 1900–1950* (Chicago: Regnery, 1951)

Flexner, Eleanor, *American Playwrights: 1918–1938* (New York: Simon and Schuster, n.d.)

Gagey, Edmond M., *Revolution in American Drama* (New York: Columbia University Press, 1947)

Nathan, George Jean, *The Morning After the First Night* (New York: Knopf, 1938)

Rabkin, Gerald, *Drama and Commitment* (Bloomington: Indiana University Press, 1964)

ELMER RICE

Durham, Frank, *Elmer Rice* (New York: Twayne, 1970)

Elwood, William R., 'An Interview with Elmer Rice on Expressionism', *Educational Theatre Journal*, 20 (March 1968), 1–7

Hogan, Robert, *The Independence of Elmer Rice* (Carbondale: Southern Illinois University Press, 1965)

Rice, Elmer, *The Living Theatre* (New York: Harper and Brothers, 1959)

——, *Minority Report* (New York: Simon and Schuster, 1963)

Valgemae, Mardi, *Accelerated Grimace* (Carbondale: Southern Illinois University Press, 1972)

E. E. CUMMINGS

Cohn, Ruby, *Dialogue in American Drama* (Bloomington: Indiana University Press, 1971)

Cummings, E. E., *i: six nonlectures* (Cambridge: Harvard University Press, 1977)

——, *A Miscellany*, George J. Firmage (ed.) (New York: Argophile Press, 1958)

Dukore, Bernard F. and Daniel C. Gerould, 'A Mirror Surrounded by Mirrors: E. E. Cummings' *Him*', *Players*, 44 (December 1968–January 1969), 54–6.

Friedman, Norman, *E. E. Cummings* (Carbondale: Southern Illinois University Press, 1964)

Him and the Critics (New York: Provincetown Players, 1928)

Kennedy, Richard S., *Dreams in the Mirror* (New York: Liveright, 1980)

Selected Bibliography

GEORGE S. KAUFMAN AND MOSS HART

Goldstein, Malcolm, *George S. Kaufman* (New York: Oxford University Press, 1977)

Hart, Moss, *Act One* (New York: Signet, 1960)

Teichmann, Howard, *George S. Kaufman* (New York: Atheneum, 1972)

MAXWELL ANDERSON

Anderson, Maxwell, *Off Broadway: Essays about the Theatre* (New York: Sloane, 1947).

Avery, Leonard G. (ed.), *Dramatist in America* (Chapel Hill: University of North Carolina Press, 1977)

Bailey, Mabel B., *Maxwell Anderson* (New York: Abelard-Schuman, 1957)

Jones, John B., 'Shakespeare as Myth and the Structure of *Winterset*', *Educational Theatre Journal*, 25 (March 1973), 34–45

Shivers, Alfred S., *Maxwell Anderson* (Boston: Twayne, 1976)

Thompson, Alan R., *The Anatomy of Drama* (Berkeley: University of California Press, 1946)

CLIFFORD ODETS

Brenman-Gibson, Margaret, *Clifford Odets* (New York: Atheneum, 1981)

Cantor, Harold, *Clifford Odets: Playwright-Poet* (Metuchen, N.J.: Scarecrow Press, 1978)

Clurman, Harold, *The Fervent Years* (New York: Hill and Wang, 1967)

Goldstein, Malcolm, *The Political Stage* (New York: Oxford University Press, 1974)

Kazin, Alfred, *Starting Out in the Thirties* (Boston: Little, Brown, 1965)

Mendelsohn, Michael J., *Clifford Odets: Humane Dramatist* (Deland, Florida: Everett Edwards, 1969)

Odets, Clifford, 'How a Playwright Triumphs', *Harper's Magazine*, 233 (September 1964), 64–74

Shuman, R. Baird, *Clifford Odets* (New York: Twayne, 1962)
Warshow, Robert, *The Immediate Experience* (New York: Atheneum, 1971)

THORNTON WILDER

Burbank, Rex, *Thornton Wilder* (New York: Twayne, 1978)
Goldstein, Malcolm, *The Art of Thornton Wilder* (Lincoln: University of Nebraska Press, 1965)
Haberman, Donald, *The Plays of Thornton Wilder* (Middletown, Conn.: Wesleyan University Press, 1969)
Porter, Thomas E., *Myth and Modern American Drama* (Wayne State University Press, 1969)
Scott, Winfield Townley, *Exiles and Fabrications* (Garden City, N.Y.: Doubleday, 1971)
Wilder, Amos Niven, *Thornton Wilder and His Public* (Philadelphia: Fortress Press, 1980)
Wilder, Thornton, *American Characteristics and Other Essays*, Donald Gallup (ed.) (New York: Harper and Row, 1979)

LILLIAN HELLMAN

Falk, Doris V., *Lillian Hellman* (New York: Ungar, 1978)
Hellman, Lillian, *Pentimento* (Boston: Little, Brown, 1973)
Lederer, Katherine, *Lillian Hellman* (Boston: Twayne, 1979)
Moody, Richard, *Lillian Hellman: Playwright* (New York: Pegasus, 1972)

WILLIAM SAROYAN

Floan, Howard R., *William Saroyan* (New York: Twayne, 1966)
Saroyan, William, *I Used to Believe I Had Forever Now I'm Not So Sure* (New York: Cowles, 1968)
——, *The Time of Your Life and Other Plays* (New York: Bantam, 1967)

Index

185

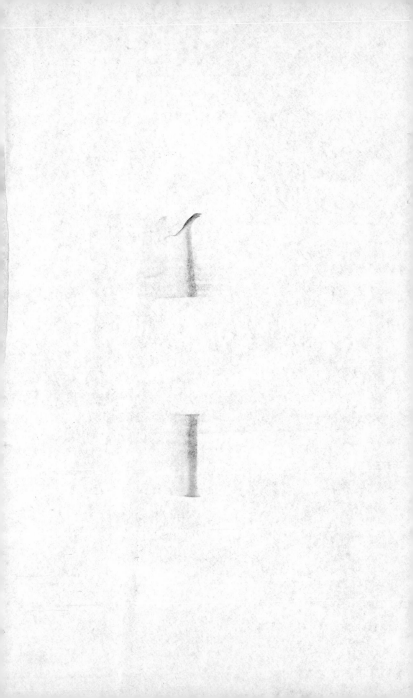